SOMERSET CENTENARIANS

The Somerset Care Group
20th ANNIVERSARY YEAR

KALINA NEWMAN

HALSGROVE

First published in Great Britain in 2011

Copyright © 2011 Somerset Care

British Library Cataloguing-in-Publication Data
A CIP record for this title is available from the British Library

ISBN 978 0 85704 080 0

HALSGROVE
Halsgrove House,
Ryelands Business Park,
Bagley Road, Wellington, Somerset TA21 9PZ
Tel: 01823 653777   Fax: 01823 216796
email: sales@halsgrove.com

Part of the Halsgrove group of companies
Information on all Halsgrove titles is available at: www.halsgrove.com

Printed in China by Everbest Printing Co Ltd

CONTENTS

ACKNOWLEDGEMENTS

THIS BOOK IS THE result of the collaboration and co-operation of many individuals, all of whom gave their time to help share the stories of our centenarians.

Firstly and most importantly we must thank the centenarians themselves, who shared their memories with Kalina Newman to enable her to write the chapters. In many instances family members accompanied their relatives on these interviews and supplemented their stories with their own recollections, as well as supplying their own archive photographs. We thank them for their time in doing this.

Harry Patch's chapter was written from the perspective of his great friend Nick Fear; Fletcher House Manager Carol Mohide; and the staff who knew him. Our thanks go to them and also to Jim Ross, who supplied the eulogy delivered at Harry's funeral, extracts of which are included.

For many reasons not all of our centenarians had photographs of their own, and we would like to extend our thanks to those people and organisations not related to the subjects who so willingly and enthusiastically provided photographs for us. Particular thanks are due to Tim Crumplin, Archive Manager at Clarks, who located and supplied archive images of Clarks Shoe Factory in Street and of Hilda Goulding's husband; and to the Mid Somerset Series for photographs of Harry Patch.

The process of identifying people willing to take part in the book, discussing the idea with them, and gaining all necessary approvals was no small feat and our thanks go to the Managers at our care homes and community care bases for adding this task to their already busy schedules.

The production of this book has been a team effort by Somerset Care staff. Special thanks go to the project team of Hannah Rowe, Jane Lynch and Sue Wilson for all their diligent work in steering the project, sourcing photographs and other material, editing and co-ordinating the contributions of many others.

Our final thanks go to our staff group of more than 4,000 whose dedication to the people we care for makes it possible for our centenarians, and those approaching this milestone, to enjoy their longevity to the greatest extent possible.

FOREWORD

Somerset Centenarians
Joan Bakewell

I HAVE ALWAYS known that simply looking at people who have lived a long time, gives you no clue as to what their lives have been like and what they themselves have experienced. These accounts remedy that. Here are the records of lives that began well before World War 1. And what a wealth of intriguing stories they have to tell.

There is no better way of transforming our attitude to the old than in listening to what they have to tell us. We know from the history books that life was tough at the start of the twentieth century. But it is the detail we have in these accounts that is so telling. Here are tales of family discipline - no elbows on the dining table - and the habit of Sunday Schools every weekend. We are reminded how important the job of tailor was, when there were no department stores or High Street chains providing clothes off the peg. We learn about the impeccable style of the Tiller girls and the harsh moral judgements on a child born out of wedlock. There is laughter and tears throughout these stories. They remind us the lives of the old were rich and varied, and there are more and more among us who are living to leave a similar legacy.

This book will do much to revise the view society takes of the old. It is an important step in giving real presence to individual lives. Old people deserve to be heard: we are the richer from hearing them.

INTRODUCTION

Andrew Larpent OBE, Chief Executive of Somerset Care

WE ALL HAVE DAYS and significant anniversaries throughout our lives that are filled with memories. One of these occurred for me on 26th October 2010. On that day I was in the US city of Portland, Oregon participating in an international study tour of some of America's ageing services facilities and retirement communities. Along with 22 fellow professional care executives, I was enjoying the opportunity to meet many delightful, active and welcoming older Americans, in their nineties and older, who are still living out their American Dream supported by caring people and caring organisations. As we travelled through the spectacular scenery of the US West Coast states in their rich autumn colours, I was somewhat distracted and my thoughts were of my late father who, had he lived, would on that day have attained the age of 100. My thoughts were of a wonderful man who enjoyed life and to whom I owe so much, and of his untimely death back in 1977.

The loss of a parent is always a hard thing to endure and, over the last 33 years, I have frequently thought of the adult conversations and the grown up relationship that my father's premature death denied us. His own life came to an end when, at the age of 67 and after years of ill health exacerbated by the deprivations he endured on wartime service in Burma, his heart gave out. Later that year his grandson, my eldest son, was born and sadly none of my children ever got to meet him. So the day of the 100th anniversary of his birth in 1910 was, for me, a day of poignant memories.

This personal bereavement experience is one that is shared by many people who are denied the enrichment to their lives that parental longevity can bring. The opportunities to grow older together, to share stories, to experience the interaction of generations within families, to watch children grow and to share lives is a precious gift enjoyed by many, desired by most and denied to many more. Old age can for many be a time of rich fulfillment and pleasure in the autumn of our years and it is a time we all hope to be able to enjoy.

Frequently though the challenges of physical infirmity or mental frailty conspire to obscure the positive aspects of ageing. Old age is no picnic for many in our society and its appearance on the horizon of our lives can be a cause for anxiety and worry. How will I manage when I can't get about as I want to? Will my money run out? Who will look after me? Will I be a burden on others? Will they put me in a home? Who cares?

In this field of conflicting emotions, contradictions and challenges associated with ageing, Somerset Care has been working since its creation by Somerset County Council back in 1991. Building on many years of public service experience prior to its formation, the Company has been developing its services and building its reputation as one of the country's leading care services organisations. In 2011 we mark the first twenty years of our existence with a sense of pride and of

Edith Wilkinson and Hilda Goulding

Residential care at Cary
Brook, Castle Cary.

Over 45,000 hours of community
care are provided every week.

continued commitment to Somerset residents, whose elected Council brought about the formation of the Company. To mark this important milestone we have chosen to celebrate the people of Somerset and particularly its growing contingent of centenarians. They provide our inspiration and help us to define our mission. We are most grateful to our centenarians who have consented to tell their stories. They and the lives they have led and in many cases are continuing to lead are the subject of this book. We thank them for sharing their lives and their stories with us.

THE SOMERSET CARE GROUP

The story of the Somerset Care Group over the past twenty years is the story of the development of a modern form of business model that is now becoming increasingly a beacon for the future of public service provision in the United Kingdom. The Company was created by Somerset County Council in 1991, on behalf of and for the benefit of the people of Somerset. The decision was a brave and innovative response at the time to the need for greater efficiency in the delivery of public services. Somerset was the first county to outsource all its care provision for older people in this way. Since 1991 other counties have made similar moves, but none have developed a model of public service social enterprise as comprehensive or as successful as Somerset Care. The Company is unique in its position as a commercial not-for-profit organisation, committed in perpetuity to the county in which it originated.

While rooted firmly in Somerset the Company has grown significantly in the past twenty years and it now provides services across a wide geographical area of the South and South West of England. Our services include residential and nursing homes, many with specialist facilities for people living with dementia. Our care homes offer modern care services in home settings that are rooted in, and very much supported by, the communities they serve. Many of our homes employ and serve multiple generations from the same families. In this way we see the Company as a provider of essential community services. Our care homes enjoy a strong reputation and are highly valued by the communities they serve. The care services provided by our staff represents and demonstrates some of the best qualities of life in our rural county of Somerset.

In addition to our care homes the Group is also a major provider of domiciliary care services to people living in their own homes. Throughout Somerset and in 14 other local authority areas throughout southern England the Group delivers some 45,000 hours of home care services every week of the year. It is a large and growing service that has grown steadily every year since Somerset Care was formed, as we seek to provide the essential care and support services on which so many older people and younger disabled adults depend. Our staff are out serving their communities at all times and in all weathers ensuring that people are able to continue to live safely and securely in their own homes for as long as they wish to do so. This is local care, by local people for local people.

CENTENARIANS – LIVING WITH LONGEVITY

In 1952, the first year of her reign, Queen Elizabeth II agreed to continue the established tradition that the sovereign should send a telegram to citizens who attained the age of 100. That year she sent out 255 messages of congratulations. Telegrams have, since 1999, been replaced by birthday greetings cards and the annual numbers sent by Her Majesty are now in the thousands. The demographic statistics of ageing throughout the world tell an amazing story of accelerating longevity. It is a social reality that is confronting and worrying governments across the world. It is also a trend that has been set by our own Royal Family in the person of Queen Elizabeth the Queen Mother, who celebrated her own 100th birthday on 4th August 2000.

Centenarians are the fastest growing age group in our society and increasing numbers of older people are now living well into their eleventh decade. The numbers are set to increase rapidly as medical science continues to offer greater opportunities to extend lives. It is estimated that by the middle of the century there will be approximately half a million centenarians living in the United Kingdom. Female centenarians have always outnumbered male centenarians, but the ratio has fallen in recent years. Since 2000 the estimated number of male centenarians has more than doubled from 700 to 1,700 in 2009, while the number of female centenarians increased by 62 per cent from 6,100 to 9,900.

The fact that people are living longer is primarily a cause for celebration and this book is our contribution to celebrating the great social opportunity that this gives to so many of us. In 2010 Somerset Care was providing care and support to over 30 centenarians in our care homes and to an equal number living in their own homes in the community. Our commitment is to help to enable everyone to enjoy their longevity to the greatest extent possible. 100th birthday parties in our homes are now common occurrences and each is celebrated in as much style as is possible for the individual concerned. Our Somerset Centenarians are our Somerset treasures and it is they who inspire and motivate all those of us who are privileged to support them.

The Queen Mother at 100.

THE 'TELL YOUR STORY' PROJECT

At Somerset Care we believe that every person who we support in one of our care homes or in the community is an individual, with their own personality and unique background. Personal dignity and self respect are values to which we give very high priority. We believe that everyone has a story to tell about their lives and about things that matter to them, and through our work with those we support and their families we want to enable all who are willing to do so to tell and take pride in their own story in a way that works for them.

We recognise that not all stories are those of happiness, harmony and success, and you will see that in the stories we are about to share with you. Many lack the satisfying conclusion of a happy ending. Many evoke memories and experiences that can be painful and difficult to contemplate. For this reason we take care with our residents and clients in the community to try to identify aspects of lives lived that, while not denying negative episodes, will tend, in the words of the song, towards the desire to "accentuate the positive".

The best way we can support people to 'Tell Their Stories' is by engagement with families and friends, as we often find that younger members of families know little about the lives and stories of older generations. The process of researching, developing and telling the story can do much to enhance the respect younger people have for their elders, and their pride in the achievements of senior generations.

Storytelling is about imagination, creativity and teamwork. We believe that this powerful theme has the potential greatly to enhance the quality of life for older people and particularly those with any form of memory loss. It is a way to offer stimulation, interest and enjoyment both for the subjects of the stories and for those who care about them. Storytelling is an activity best conducted by groups of people working together. In our care settings we see the group as the individual, the family and friends, supported by the care staff.

We see the powerful intergenerational effects, particularly amongst younger people, of engaging with the life stories of their parents, grandparents and elders. It remains the case today that family and group identity and cohesion is stronger in communities where the oral storytelling tradition remains strong. In indigenous populations, where the sophistication, materialism and pace of life is less frenetic than that in our developed cultures, it is the power of the storytelling tradition that helps elders within communities to retain their status and positions of dignity, wisdom and respect.

Much of our work in this field has taken us into the field of "Digital Storytelling". By making use of readily accessible new media technology we encourage families and younger people to assist in the creation of life story DVDs about the lives of older people. The techniques are easy to learn and the power of such stories in assisting older people to retain their self respect and dignity as their personal mental capacity declines is significant.

My introduction to the power of digital storytelling came from a close friendship that my wife and I developed with our close neighbours in our village of Over Stratton in South Somerset. Ron and Kate Tucker both passed away within months of each other in 2009. They were a close and devoted couple who became much more than neighbours to us. Three years before she died Kate was presented, on her 90th birthday, with a DVD about her life that had been created by her daughter Judi. Judi Tucker lives in Sydney, Australia, where she runs her own media company. Using old photos from the family album, clips of home movies, Kate's favourite music and her own voice recounting fond memories, Judi was able to create a means of giving Kate back her memory. The DVD was a source of great comfort and pleasure for Kate, who watched it regularly and shared it with friends through the last years of her life.

Students are involved in the 'Tell Your Story' project, promoting understanding between the generations.

In pursuit of our work in this field I applied in 2009 for a Travel Fellowship with the Winston Churchill Memorial Trust, in order to study storytelling and its application in the field of dementia care and support. The resulting award gave me the opportunity to travel to Canada and the United States in 2010 to explore the world of storytelling in those countries. In 2011 I have a further trip planned to Australia and New Zealand. This has offered the opportunity to meet many people engaged in this work in academic institutions and care settings, to understand better the power of storytelling, and in particular to draw lessons from the oral storytelling tradition that is still strongly maintained in indigenous cultures. In October 2010 I was able to spend some time with the wonderful team at the Centre for Digital Storytelling in Berkeley, California. The work that is being undertaken at this small centre in promoting and developing this modern art form is inspirational, and demonstrated clearly to me the power this application of new media technologies has to transform and enrich lives.

The "Tell Your Story" theme has now been adopted throughout the Somerset Care Group. Together with our friends and colleagues at the Department of Psychology at Exeter University we are undertaking a research project to understand better the ways in which life story work can contribute to improvements in the sense of self, well-being, cognition and mental acuity amongst people living with dementia. We are now working with Media Studies students from Bridgwater

College on a project that connects them with our care home residents for the purpose of creating digital life stories.

What is quite clear from our work in this field is that storytelling is good for you. It is also fun and immensely rewarding. We believe that no-one comes to Somerset Care without a story and we will work to help as many as are willing to do so to tell their story and to enjoy passing to others their lifetimes of experiences and memories.

Andrew Larpent helps Harry Patch cut the turf at Somerset Care's new Central Office, 2003.

OUR INSPIRATION – HARRY PATCH

The inspiration to create this book of stories of Somerset Centenarians has come from our work supporting many thousands of Somerset residents over the past twenty years. Of these many wonderful people there is one who stands in our memory as our model resident, and as the outstanding representative of his generation. Harry Patch was a resident at Fletcher House in Wells for the last twelve years of his life until he passed peacefully away on 25th July 2009 at the magnificent age of 111. Harry was literally a "legend in his own lifetime" and his story forms the twentieth of our collection in this book.

Why was Harry so special? He certainly made no claim to be so. His claim to fame stemmed from a few months of his life in 1916 when at the tender age of 18, and along with millions of others, he participated in the great and utterly futile battle of Passchendaele on the Western Front at the height of the First World War. He was then a Private in the Duke of Cornwall's Light Infantry. He was wounded and evacuated.

Harry went on to live his life after the war as an ordinary man of Somerset. Having long outlived his family he chose at the age of 98 to move into residential care in Fletcher House. Two years later, when he reached the age of 100, he gradually came to the attention of his community, then his county, then his nation and then the world. By the time he was 105 he was fully embarked on the third career for which he became famous, that of being a centenarian and ultimately the last surviving World War One front line veteran. During his eleventh decade of life Harry became a global celebrity. He was awarded an honorary degree by the University of Bristol where he had worked as a plumber during the construction of the Wills Memorial Building in the 1920s. He undertook visits back to the World War One battlefields. He had a poem written about him by the Poet Laureate, he became the subject of documentary films, he published his autobiography, he launched an RNLI lifeboat that was named in his honour. Above all he lived his final years to the full surrounded by the love and care of his Somerset Care family. If ever there was a testament to the enabling power of good quality residential care and the ability of the centenarian to contribute to society then surely Harry, the "ordinary man" of Somerset, and the team who supported him, must claim that honour.

Harry's story is that of an ordinary man of Somerset. His story along with the others collected in this book illustrate the lives of a representative group of Somerset people. These are ordinary people made extraordinary by their longevity. We hope that their stories will strengthen the resolve of future generations of Somerset Centenarians to keep on living life to the full. As Harry demonstrated it is never too late to start something new. In his case he became a famous celebrity. We hope to see many others following his lead in the years to come.

LESLIE MILES

'I don't like to be in the limelight … I'm a quiet man'.

KING GEORGE V had been on the throne for six months when Leslie Miles took his first gulp of air. It was December 5th 1910. He was born to Horace and Elsie Miles and two years later he had a brother called Lionel. During the war, Leslie, Lionel and their mother lived with their grand-parents as their father Horace was in the Army, stationed in France. Horace had spent most of his childhood in India as his father was in the Army and, wanting a piece of the action, he signed up when he was 14 and did what was called 'boy service'. As a young man, he was stationed on the North West Frontier in India experiencing some ferocious battles and deft cunning from Afghan soldiers. They had to put chains through rifles to prevent theft and yet when you woke up in the morning, those rifles would be gone and the cables cut. Horace was in the Army for 25 years and was an exceptional role model for young Leslie Miles.

Leslie was very bright and loved school, absorbing as much knowledge as he could with his keen young mind. Throughout his education, Leslie would attend St Mary's, the very strict Asquith Boys School and the Memorial School, which were all in Taunton. All the children would sit along a long bench at wooden tables. He always did extremely well at school as he progressed through the standards and he remembers clearly that due to being much cleverer than the other boys, which he says with enormous modesty, his master had to create a special class so he could give him lessons to do that were more advanced than the rest. This class was called X7, of which Leslie would be the only pupil. He liked all subjects especially scale drawing and once did a chalk drawing on dark grey paper of a sea shore scene, puffy white waves crashing against the shore. He also won second prize for writing an excellent essay on health, for which he was paid two shillings and six pence. He was very keen on arithmetic and thinks calculators should be banned as "in those days, we did it ourselves, with our brains. Nobody really knows how to do anything these days".

Leslie was a mischievous child and was once caught chasing a boy into the cloakroom but just as the master was about to strike him with the cane Leslie diverted his attention, pulling his hand back, making a wincing sound. The teacher believed he had struck him and let him go! He used to love playing football as a centre half and would compete against different schools, once winning a silver medal. He strongly feels that the game isn't the same and is more "a business of fabulous money than a sport". As he approached his second decade things were going to change.

D.O.B. 05/12/1910

Les's father and other bandsmen at Jellalabad Barracks in Taunton, 1918. Les is on the far right on the bench and at the other end is Ken Steele, who would later become Chief Constable of Taunton.

Group outing in the countryside. Les is about 9 or so,1919.

During the war, his father had been stationed in France and after being back a short time, it was time to leave the safety of Taunton for another adventure.

When Leslie was just nine years old, he was taken to Belfast as his father was in the First Battalion Somerset Light Infantry and six hundred men had been called up after Partition, which separated Northern Ireland from the rest of the country. By 1920 Partition had been agreed and it was into this volatile atmosphere that the young brothers were brought, and they would live in the barracks for the next eighteen months. The family were stationed a few miles out of Belfast and the barracks was huge with high iron railings that Les and his pals would squeeze their tiny bodies through, just to mess around and wander about. The barracks skirted the edge of the Danville whisky estate and the boys would hide themselves away, keeping a look out for Major Fisk, the chap who taught them and generally kept an eye on them.

BELFAST

In the nineteenth century Belfast became Ireland's leading industrial city with linen, tobacco, heavy engineering and shipbuilding dominating the economy. Sectarian tensions would start to run high and deep as migrants filtered in, especially from rural Ulster. In 1829 the parades organised by the Orange Order, a Protestant organisation linked to unionism, were banned, which led to serious rioting. Conflict and unrest would continue for decades, spreading over the whole of Ireland. In 1886 the Protestants celebrated the defeat of the Home Rule Bill, leading to even more rioting and protest marches. By 1901, Belfast was experiencing its fair share of disruption and conflict due to sectarian issues and in 1912 the Liberal Government attempted to pass the Third Home Rule Bill. Eventually partition was achieved under the Government of Ireland Act 1920, and Ireland was effectively split in half.

It was during this time that Les would see the *Olympic* set sail. She was the leading ship of the Olympic class ocean liners, built for the White Star Line which included *Titanic* and *Britannic*. She was moored at the Harland and Wolff shipbuilders.

"We spent all winter at these barracks and it snowed like anything … anyway, these barracks were a little bit high up so you had to stand on a wall and look over and there was Belfast Docks … you know, the entrance to Belfast harbour. Well early one morning, I came out of the married quarters with my dad and we were walking down toward the daylight and there were these huge railings, six or eight feet high, and I saw this massive ship going out to sea. Anyway, the word had gone round the town, it was a well known thing, it were the *Olympic*. Well, being a nipper, you didn't really realise what a big thing it was, not until later".

OLYMPIC

Launched on October 20 1910, she was identical to *Titanic* and was sailed under the command of Captain E. J. Smith, who would later take charge of *Titanic's* maiden voyage to New York on June 14 1911. As *Britannic* sank during the war, *Olympic* was the only survivor out of the three. Construction began three months before *Titanic* with the keel being laid in December 1908 and the hull was painted in light grey for photographic purposes, as it made lines cleaner in black and white photographs. *Olympic* consumed 650 tons of coal every 24 hours with an average speed of 21.7 knots on her maiden voyage. The *Olympic* had few mishaps and was remembered fondly by crew member Violet Jessop, who not only survived the collision with British warship HMS *Hawke*, but also *Titanic* and the 1916 sinking of *Britannic*. She had many notable achievements such as the daring rescue of the battleship *Audacious*, serving as a troopship carrying Canadians to the war front, and sinking the German submarine U-103, becoming the only merchant ship to sink an enemy warship during the war. In 1920, she returned to passenger service and her last voyage ended in Southampton on April 12 1935. If you visit the White Swan in Alnwick, you may spy some of her fixtures and fittings.

Early in 1921, the Miles family moved back to Taunton as Les's father was looking forward to his retirement from the Army and reviving his role as a band sergeant. Les continued with his schooling, and in his spare time he would have numerous adventures with his pals. When he was fifteen, he built a radio from scratch, carefully following the detailed diagrams in a weekly periodical called *Practical Wireless* whilst listening to BBC World Service. It was at this time that Les Miles chanced upon a good job. He had always enjoyed tinkering with cars and it so happened that his father had an army colleague, Colonel Badcock, who was a director at the Taunton Motor Company. Les was taken on as an apprentice coach trimmer, responsible for putting all the upholstery in the cars, but was soon transferred to the assembly department. The first cars he worked on were wooden and then as he became more experienced and the times changed, he moved onto pressed steel.

There was good camaraderie amongst his workmates despite some being brash Londoners that Les tolerated. He became great friends with a local boy called Fred Paul and they would lark around and visit friends in North Curry, attend Wilton church regularly, and walk out with pretty girls. The family remained very close and one summer afternoon, Leslie, his father and brother Lionel were out enjoying a country walk when they spotted a Zeppelin overhead. No longer used as reconnaissance aircraft, this was a passenger airship but they discovered afterwards that it was covertly being used by the Germans for espionage purposes.

ZEPPELIN

A type of rigid airship, it was pioneered by Count Ferdinand Von Zeppelin in the early twentieth Century. It was patented in the United States on 14th March 1899. Before the outbreak of WW1 the Zeppelins were operated by DELAG, the first commercial airline, serving scheduled flights. The first Zeppelin flight was on 2 July 1900 over Lake Constance, which lasted 18 minutes, and in 1909 the LZ6 became the first airship to be used for commercial passenger transport. Once the war started the German military made extensive use of the Zeppelins as bombers and scouts and the advantages of the impressive machine were speed, greater range and more space for guns and bombs. The disadvantage was its vulnerability to incendiary ammunition. The main use was reconnaissance missions over the North Sea and the Baltic, where they were able to spy on allied vessels and prevent British ships approaching Germany amongst other duties. Between 1915 and

Les and Lionel larking about in the sea, 1928.

Les and Phyllis'
wedding day, 1935.

1918, the German Navy and Army Air services directed a number of strategic raids against Britain. The Zeppelin era came to an end on May 6 1937 when LZ129 Hindenburg filled with hydrogen and burst into flames, killing many on board.

It was on a lovely sunny day early in 1931 that Les Miles met the girl he would marry. Les, Lionel and some friends had gone to Watchet harbour on the steam train and they'd had a happy day larking around but on the way home there were so many people packed on the train that they all squeezed into the luggage carriage, which was full of girls in summer dresses. It so happened that Lionel knew some of these girls and introduced everyone. It was Leslie's lucky day, as a pretty girl called Phyllis seemed quite keen to chat to him and they spent the rest of the journey engrossed in each other's company. After courting for 3 or 4 years, Phyllis got tired of waiting and exclaimed one day, "Hey, Les! Why don't us get wed? " They married in 1935 in Trinity church, Taunton and their first home together was a rented flat in a nice big house in Victoria Street, owned by a lady called Mrs Berryman, who owned a corsetiere shop in Bath Place. The small flat was reached by climbing a broad oak staircase which Les carried his bride up, taking the stairs two at a time. Leslie continued to work for the Taunton Motor Company whilst Phyllis found work ironing and pressing razor sharp creases along the cuffs and collars of starched cotton shirts. The factory was owned by the White brothers, famous in the area for racing albino pigeons and who could always be found sipping a pint of ale in the Railway Tavern. For the next few years they lived a happy comfortable life in Taunton, moving from time to time but generally enjoying their life together. Then World War Two broke out.

During the war, Les's job was put on hold and he was found a reserve occupation which helped contribute to the war effort, and he moved to Filton near Bristol to work for the Bristol Aeroplane Company. By the time Les went to work for the company and be part of the 4,200 strong workforce, they were ready to take on the rearmament programme ordered by the government. When war broke out, the Bristol Aeroplane Company was the largest single aircraft manufacturing unit in the world. Les' first job was making small fittings in a large workshop where he made friends with Frank Packer, a wiry plasterer from Newcastle. They were then transferred together to the erecting hall where the fuselages were made and Leslie Miles was there, reporting for duty and would be actively involved in the building and manufacturing of one of Britain's most important wartime aircraft, the Beaufighter. Leslie continued to work for the British Aeroplane Company until the end of the war and due to its production of highly elite aircraft, the units and workshops became a sought after target for the German bombers and Les experienced many terrifying bombing raids. Once they bombed the factory quite badly causing the men to run for their lives but the second time the Germans tried it, they were chased away by British Spitfires.

" Almost every night they would drop bombs but this day was a more concentrated raid as they were determined to wipe out the production of planes. Anyway, after the raid was over the boss says, 'you all go home for the rest of the day'. Well, we all waited for the bus and there were hundreds working at the company so they had laid on loads of buses. So, we were travelling home and the branches of a tree touched the top deck … well, instantly everyone dropped to the floor."

Jackie as a baby, 1962.

BRISTOL AEROPLANE COMPANY

The British and Colonial Aeroplane Company was founded in 1910 by Sir George White to manufacture aircraft at Filton near Bristol. The initial venture was an improvised version of the Voisin Brothers' Zodiac 'Boxkite' biplane but it never flew and the first successful design was the Bristol Boxkite. The Royal Aeroplane Club was created soon after and was regarded as the best in the world between 1910 and 1914. During this time, a formidable aeronautical engineer called Frank Barnwell created the Bristol Scout, one of the first fighter planes to enter British service, then later came the backbone of the Royal Air Force, the Bristol Fighter. In 1920, the Bristol Aeroplane Company was born and, over the next few years, was to create some of the most awesome flying machines. The British Bulldog Fighter formed the mainstay of RAF fighters between 1918 and 1935, noted for the policy of all-steel airframes, powered by Bristol engines. During the Second World War, the Beaufighter was Bristol's most important aircraft.

BEAUFIGHTER

The name derived from the Beaufort Fighter and it was a long range fighter, night fighter, ground attack aircraft and torpedo bomber combining the wings, undercarriage, engines and tail plane of the Beaufort, with a much slimmer fuselage, to produce a lighter aircraft. It first flew on July 17 1939 with Captain Unwins at the control. The Beaufighter had speed and firepower and once it had detected a German BF110 night stalker it would respond with audacious power. It had served in all theatres of war and performed particularly well in the Western Desert. Thanks to their long range, when the last Beaufighter left the Weston Super Mare works on September 21 1945, a total of 5,562 aircraft of this type had been produced in the UK. During its operational career, it had played a prime role in defeating the Luftwaffe's night 'Blitz' of 1940-1941 and had operated in every significant campaign of the war.

These unpredictable war years were quite an upheaval for Phyllis, who had initially found lodgings with Mrs Blizzard in Bristol until they had the opportunity to rent a house in Filton, where they would stay for the next seven years. During the war, Phyllis became pregnant with

Below left: A car on the forecourt, emblazoned with the Allens logo.

Below centre: Les and two friends at work at Allens, 1950s.

Below right: Les and Alfie Maycock at work at Allens, 1950s.

her first child and was therefore exempt from doing her duties for the war effort. It was to be a very difficult birth and a top Bristol gynaecologist was called in to help deliver the baby. Les decided after the trauma of childbirth he would never put Phyllis through this again, and Jacqueline was to be their only child. The dangers of war were even more accentuated with a small baby. It seemed you never knew when you were going to be bombed as the Germans were unpredictable, missing certain nights to lull you into a false calm. The family would shelter under the stairs and had built an Anderson shelter by digging a semi dugout in the garden and erecting the structure over it. They would make do as best they could whilst most things were rationed. Les used to get chocolate from the Americans and Phyllis would create magical things with dried egg, mixing it with water and then frying it so the yolk looked broken. Leslie would also tend his allotment and grow potatoes, runner beans, carrots and onions. It was also preferable to share car journeys to preserve fuel which was handy for Les as he never learnt to drive, preferring to cycle. By the mid Forties, the war was coming to an end and it was time for the family to move back to Taunton. It wasn't long though before Leslie heard of a better job with rival firm Allens and, as the 1950s approached, Les was on the move. He would work in the motor trade for the next thirty five years. When Les retired he did not remain idle, continuing to work for Allens as a valet, keeping the cars neat and tidy. Les always loved his bike and cycled everywhere until he was well into his nineties.

After the war, as the Fifties approached, Les and Phyllis moved in with her parents. Jackie embarked on her first year at school and eventually the family got a council house in St Alban's Close. Life in Taunton was quiet but happy. The family got together whenever they could and Les saw Lionel from time to time as he lived on the other side of town. The normality of everyday things was a welcome change to the disruption of the war years. Les was to take up amateur photography and became a keen gardener. After leaving school, Jackie became an apprentice hairdresser, only to give up her job at 18 to marry Roy as he was called up to do his National Service. If you were married you didn't have to go overseas so he signed up and went into the Air Force.

It was the early Sixties when Jackie left the family home, leaving a gaping hole in Les and Phyllis' life. They adored their daughter and life would never be quite the same despite the fact

Right: Les and Phyllis at the Howard Davis Park, St. Helier, Jersey. Summer holidays, July 1965.

Far right: Les, Phyllis, Doris (her sister) and Maurice on holidays, 1960.

Far left: The family enjoy a post lunch respite outside Jackie's house in Obridge, 1986.

Left: Les and granddaughter Shelley, 2006.

they loved each other's company. They made up for the quietness in the house by joining the Rowbarton Methodist Church's Friendship Club which introduced them to a whole new social scene. They would enjoy day trips away on the Berry's coach and holidays to Jersey but did not venture further afield until later in the Seventies, when they would take holidays abroad with Phyllis' sister Doris and her husband Maurice. Over the years they visited Malta, Switzerland, France and Italy and these are memories that they cherished later in life, especially when Phyllis started to lose her eyesight.

The next few years were a time for family and friends and day trips now involved the grandchildren, Darren and Shelley. The summer heat-wave of 1976 was so hot that the inside walls were roasting and the roads were shimmering. The family spent a blistering hot day at Burnham on Sea and experienced a swarm of ladybirds, enough to turn the windows of the car black. When the weather turned colder, Christmas Day would be spent at Jackie's with a real spruce and piles of presents under the tree. The whole family would remain close, visiting each other regularly and most Sundays everyone would get together for lunch, catching up with all the latest news.

In 2004, Phyllis became ill and had to go into a nursing home. They were both still living on their own in their house. Phyllis' eyesight was fairly bad and she couldn't really see properly to do the cooking so she showed Les how to cook so he could look after himself if anything happened to her. Phyllis passed away four years ago and Les stayed at home for another year until he had a fall and broke his wrist. It wasn't long before he made the decision to move to Moorhaven. When he lost his wife his world imploded and he tells me how difficult it was but he was philosophical and commented that, "it happens to all of us. It just comes to us and you get through. You deal with it." Leslie Miles is never short of visitors at Moorhaven and makes his presence felt. His daughter visits regularly, as do his grandchildren, who are now in their thirties. Les doesn't see them as much as he would like as they live very busy lives, but feels he's blessed with more than most.

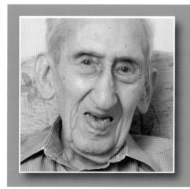

GWENDOLINE BETTS

'I'm a dancer ... I've danced all my life'

D.O.B. 04/04/1909

GWEN WAS BORN on Barrington Road, Brixton on April 4th, 1909 and had three siblings, Muriel, Hugh and Vivian. Her father's name was Simmonds and he was a rubber plantation manager who spent a lot of time away from home in Africa. Gwen would always have fond memories of him and was very close to him as a child, but due to his constant absence a strain was put on his relationship with Gwen's mother Violet. Before Gwen and the children came along, Violet was an actress starring in many silent films and worked for the Samuelson Brothers.

BERTIE SAMUELSON 1888 - 1947

A pioneer of early cinema, Samuelson started out as a Lancashire cinema exhibitor before the onset of 'talkies' and built up the Samuelson Group, the largest film equipment servicing company in the world. Born in Southport, he created Southall studios, one of the first film processing companies in the UK. In 1913, he produced an epic about the reign of Queen Victoria called *Sixty Years a Queen*, which he financed and helped produce at Ealing Studios. The following year, he bought Worton Hall in Isleworth and converted it into film studios and his first production was Conan Doyle's *A Study in Scarlet*, which was a great success in the UK and sold to the US for a four-figure sum. Following the outbreak of WW1, he produced a fictitious newsreel called *The European War Day to Day*, which played to record audiences. He then went on to shoot several sentimental dramas based on literary classics such as *Little Women* and J.M.Barrie's *The Admiral Crichton*. He amassed a regular group of players and later productions were directed by Alexander Butler. The immediate post war period was fairly difficult for the British Film Industry, mainly due to competition from growing film production in America.

Violet Simmonds was the archetypal matriarch and a force to be reckoned with. She worked until she was in her seventies as a housekeeper and cook. For all her toughness, she brought up five children marvellously, making sure they didn't want for anything. After spending a year in Whitstable living in a wooden bungalow, the family moved to Twickenham for a long period of time. During this time Gwen and the other children went to a little private school in London. There came a point when Simmonds faded from their lives and Violet met Alexander Butler, who

Right: Violet, Hugh, Gwen and Bud, 1930

Far right: Gwen in *Cheap Trips*, Royal Theatre, Exeter 1925

Publicity shot of Gwen in a beautiful long dress, 1929

worked for the Samuelson Brothers. They started a relationship which continued for many years, with Violet giving birth to a son called Bud. Gwen's sister Vivian left the family early due to an out of wedlock pregnancy and she was excluded from the family for 40 years. Gwen's mother would bring up the child, Dinah, as her own, and Gwen would never mention her sister's name. It wasn't until many years later that Dinah would discover who her real mother was.

Due to her involvement in the film industry, Violet encouraged her children to follow in her footsteps from an early age. It seemed that showbusiness really was in the blood. Violet's sister, Dolly, had made her name in America and had a son called Les, who had starred in the original *War of the Worlds* and was a popular chat show host. It was said that he had the most recognisable voice in America aside from President Roosevelt. Gwen had her first foray into showbusiness at the age of three, followed by her sister Muriel. As the girls were still quite young, there were contracts that insisted they were not permitted on stage after 10 pm. They were paid eight pounds and ten shillings on a "No Play, No Pay" basis. Over the next few years Gwen would appear in a handful of silent films, mostly made by Bertie Samuelson, who gave her these opportunities in the industry due to his friendship with Violet.

At the age of 10, Gwen performed on stage at The Old Vic with Lillian Baylis, playing an angel. The year after she appeared in the silent film, *Fate's Plaything*, a 1920s drama directed by Maurits Binger and in 1925 she starred in *Wonders* at the Olympia in Shoreditch.

The next move for the family was to Isleworth where Samuelson had created his film studios at Worton Hall. Gwen became friends with Bert Howard, a builder and scout-master, who designed a poster for a show she was performing in, for which she was given a 'thanks' badge from Lord Baden Powell. Bert fell hopelessly in love with her and sent her a proposal of marriage, scrawled in pencil on a builders invoice. She declined his offer.

At around the age of 18 Gwen was doing promotion work for a theatre and saw a young Princess Elizabeth. She was to appear in *Little Women* with her stepfather directing and at the age of 21, she played *Cinderella* on stage in Blackpool. It was around this time that Gwen was to discover her real true love.

The next time Gwen Tremayne (her stage name) would appear in *Cinderella,* it would be on the stage at the Drury Lane Theatre as a Tiller girl. Gwen had always loved to dance so when she was given this opportunity she jumped at the chance. The Tiller girls were the most popular dance

Far left: Extracts from a log book of Gwen's performances.

Left: Extract – details of lodgings and names/addresses of landladies.

troupe of the time, a chorus of dancers who linked arms and could dance as one, creating precise movement. *Cinderella* was an epic production with a huge cast and very extravagant staging, featuring many big star names of the Thirties. The set was elaborate and the builders had recreated 'the enchanted lake scene' on stage, by installing a huge pool of water. There was a tunnel that ran underneath it and the girls were meant to swim through it to get to the dressing rooms. Tragically it seemed that two of the girls who were following a rope for guidance lost their way, and drowned.

Over the next six years, Gwen worked for various dance companies. It was these experiences that inspired Gwen to replicate the flamboyant costumes she wore as a Tiller in miniature and she created a fascinating collection of dolls which would provide a record of the intricate fashions of the time.

JOHN TILLER AND THE TILLER GIRLS

John Tiller was born in 1854 and was a perfectionist who had a keen interest in music. In 1885, he became the director of The Comedy Theatre in Manchester and began teaching children to dance. His early pupils would practice for hours amongst bales of cotton in one of the local warehouses in town. In 1890, he presented a quartet of children for the pantomime *Robinson Crusoe*. He carefully chose his four best girls: Dolly Grey, Tessie Lomax and twins Cissie and Lilly Smyth. They all happened to be the same height and shape. He somehow managed to achieve absolute precision, every movement perfect and every turn simultaneous. Famous for their high kicking routines, the Tillers were highly trained and their fame spread around the world. Resident venues for Tiller girls to perform were the Folies-Bergère in Paris, the London Palladium, New York's celebrated Broadway and the Blackpool Winter Gardens. The regularity of their patterns, consisting of straight lines and geometric figures, were cheered by the masses. By the late 1800s, the troupes were dancing in ballet and pantomime performances all over the world. One of the routines was the Mystic Hussar, a flamboyant extravaganza with the girls dressed as cavaliers, waving blazing swords. In 1900, he sent a troupe of girls to America and at the height of their popularity there were three Tiller lines working the theatres on Broadway. John Tiller was to open a dance school on 72nd Street which was run by Mary Reed, a Tiller from England who had been one of the Sunshine Girls. John Tiller died in 1925 in New York and Mary Reed continued the school until 1935.

All the years of dancing took their toll on Gwen's feet. She wore white satin shoes and her feet would bleed. Sometimes she would walk home barefoot in the snow because she couldn't get her shoes on. In 1936, she was encouraged to take a little rest by her touring company so took a job as an usherette at the Odeon, Isleworth. It was here that she would meet the love of her life. Bert Betts was a film projectionist at the cinema and the two met and fell in love. They were married on June 1st 1936. Gwen would never perform on stage again as early the following year she gave birth to her first child, Michael. For the next few years, Bert worked for the Odeon Group training junior projectionists, and the family led an unsettled existence moving around the country until a more permanent position came up and they rented a house in Redhill. They stayed there throughout the war until the early Sixties. Even though Bert failed to enlist, it seemed that being a projectionist was seen as a reserve occupation. It was a requirement that servicemen see films privately, as plans for imminent invasions and any other relevant news would be shown. He contributed to the war effort by joining the Home Guard and the Auxiliary Fire Service.

After the horrors of Dunkirk, there seemed to be an all-time low in Britain. The Americans were staunch allies but had yet to join the war and the Germans were just 20 miles away. There seemed to be a horrifying glut of danger. There were the V2 rockets which made no sound at all and then there was the dull drone followed by sudden silence of a V1 doodlebug, which would stop and randomly explode, terrifying the family. At one point they had their allotment blown up whilst they took cover in the Anderson and they had a table shelter which comprised a huge steel table top with heavy duty mesh sides that Gwen and Mike would hide under. At the height of the bombardment, Bert arranged for Gwen and Mike to be evacuated to York. They stayed for 18 months while the Blitz was happening, to escape the doodlebugs that were falling all around. Bert would stay behind and make his valuable contribution to the war effort. Mike has lovely

Right: Gwen and baby Mick, 1937.

Far right: Gwen and Mick in York during the war.

memories of this time with his mother, staying in a beautiful country house just outside York that belonged to the Archbishop of York and was run impeccably by Mrs Drewe, the housekeeper. It had a shady walled garden edged with fruit trees and a long curved drive. They would go boating on the River Ouse and have day trips to places like the Cadbury factory, which made Gwen smile as she remembered being in *Elsie and the Brown Bunny* when she was ten. Mike attended a local school, which he wasn't terribly keen on, but he really didn't have too many worries. The war seemed a million miles away.

In 1946 Gwen gave birth to another boy, Rodney, who would look up to his brother, but they would always remain quite distant. Over the next few years, as well as having a small baby to look after, Gwen had many part time jobs. She worked in cafés and shops but the thing that gave her most joy was running small private dance schools and putting on performances in local venues, many of which were for charity. She would take on the role of make-up artist, choreographer and costume designer, and Mike would stay up for hours helping Gwen with the outfits. Although she was never to perform on the stage again, these

Gwen applying make up to one of the girls at the Ryegate Pageant, 1953

shows gave Gwen a taste of the life she had left behind. She would run these schools until the move to Southampton and they were a great success, giving her a chance to pass on a part of her past that she excelled in.

In the summer of 1951 Bert was offered a job as chief projectionist for the Telekinema, a small cinema built especially for the Festival of Britain's South Bank Exhibition. After the war much of the country was still in ruins and the festival was a way of celebrating the nation's recovery and to promote good quality design for the reconstruction of Britain. The most important area was the South Bank, an area of old Victorian industrial buildings and railway sidings, which was transformed into the main site. Although the festival took pride in Britain's past, it looked to the future and many Londoners saw their first ever television pictures in one of the pavilions.

The following year, Bert was involved in filming the Coronation procession from one of the tall buildings that lined the route. Gwen had forgotten to give him his sandwiches that morning and had travelled to London in the hope of finding him. Amidst the huge queues and vivid colours, she caught a glimpse of the Gold State Coach, pulled by eight grey geldings. After Bert

Right: Gwen sitting in a pretty dress, Folkestone, 1957.

Far right: Gwen and Bert at a Southern Television dinner, 1965.

Family Christmas, 1984.

had finished filming the film was rushed to Heathrow and flown to Canada, to be shown in cinemas nationwide, as only a few people owned a television. After this Bert swapped his allegiance and started to work for the Rank Organisation in London and around the country. Bert also worked with Mike Todd on *Around the World in Eighty Days*, was involved in sound and lighting, and toured with musicians such as Buddy Holly, Johnny Ray and Sarah Vaughn.

Toward the end of the Fifties Mike left home, having met and married Pam. Rodney was in his teens, a self confessed daddy's boy who tagged along with Bert whenever he could. He would later join the Navy as a radio officer. This life was all to change in 1962, when Bert got a job with Southern TV in Hampshire. While Bert was working, Gwen scoured Southampton looking for places to rent and eventually found Myrtle Cottage by the river in Bursledon. They never moved again and a most treasured possession is a painting of the cottage, painted by Tom Richardson, who owned the boatyard. She still misses it dreadfully.

Life would continue at a gentle pace as Gwen settled into her new life. The village of Bursledon sat on the River Hamble, where submerged remnants of Henry VIII's fleet had found their final resting place. The picturesque qualities of the village were captured in the 1980s' BBC television series *Howard's Way* and film crews descended on Bursledon during this time. Gwen can remember being asked to take her washing off the line as it was making a shot look untidy. The days of performing were in the past, as were the dance schools, and the only times that Gwen would be a part of the showbusiness world was when she accompanied Bert to an industry dinner. It was during this period though that she would design the Tiller costumes for her dolls and she would occupy her time by doing part time work and run a small general stores, selling fresh produce. Another thing Gwen had a passion for was painting, at which she was completely self taught. From an early age, she would see something and feel the need to depict it. Her way of painting was totally unconventional and she disliked the academic rules of fine art, preferring to dab and smear with bits of old rag. She was mostly interested in adding colour, as you couldn't get colour photos in those days. She would go to the theatre and meet her favourite stars, taking their black and white postcards which she would tint, using sepia and oil paint. She continued to paint in a more traditional way until she was in her eighties and her favourites hang on her wall at Portcullis House.

The family still managed to remain close. Gwen's mother Violet lived in a small cottage nearby for the last ten years of her life and her siblings would pay occasional visits. Muriel had given up performing years before and had been married three times. She was to see her old age out in Portsmouth, being cared for by Dinah. One morning in the early Seventies, a slightly alternative creature turned up on the doorstep, wearing faded denim and braids. It was Vivian, the long lost sister. Sadly, there was no loving reunion between the sisters as Violet had talked the family out of having a sister and as much as Dinah tried to bring everyone together, Grandma kept everyone apart. The only emotional reunion was between Dinah and her mother and they would make the most of the time they had left.

Life in Bursledon was enough to keep Gwen happy and if she was not pottering round her garden or serving sticky cake and Ceylon tea in fine china, she would go and spend time in the family caravan on Ruby Road in Bitterne. She didn't drive so she would take the bus, which meandered slowly down country lanes. She loved her own company and would stay for days and weeks at a time, with only Shep, the golden retriever, for company. She took her paints to capture red poppies and sunsets. The evenings were often spent with Pearl, a younger woman she'd met whilst doing part time work in the site shop. Pearl still remains a great friend now.

Even after he retired Bert was never idle which meant that Gwen had much time to herself. He set up a business renting TV equipment for various events; worked at Southampton Docks immigration office and then in the early Nineties he became a school governor, running regattas and committees. The couple rarely saw each other, apart from meals which he would eat quickly as he had somewhere to go. He tried to encourage her to attend all the social activities that his life entailed and although she enjoyed certain occasions, she preferred a quieter existence.

In 2003 Bert passed away after a year of illness during which Gwen had nursed him. Although she missed him and was very fond of him, she accepted that they had grown apart in later life. Bert thought the world of her but she sometimes found it hard to show her emotions. Gwen continued to live in the cottage alone but it became obvious that she could not manage and was in fact becoming more of a danger to herself, so she went to live with Mike. It was only a matter of time before Mike took the very difficult decision to move his mother to Portcullis House. This is something that he feels terribly guilty for as his mother constantly tells him how much she misses the cottage by the river. He has made her room as warm and familiar as Myrtle Cottage, surrounding her with everything she holds dear.

Gwen feeding the ducks at the end of her garden (River Hamble), 1989.

ANNIE ISHERWOOD

'A postmaster's wife, who was born in Lancashire
but followed the romance of life on Exmoor'

ANNIE ISHERWOOD was born on 22 September 1910, in Bury, a market town located in the foothills of the western Pennines. The family lived in a modest red bricked house on Marsden Street with three decent sized bedrooms and a bathroom with an overhead shower, which was a luxury in those days as most had tin baths in the kitchen. Along the side and tucked at the back were well kept gardens and small allotments. Annie had a middle class upbringing and was the only child of Robert and Hannah Mary Bentley. She always regretted not having any brothers and sisters and her earliest memory is going to the promenade at Blackpool and building sandcastles with other children, which made her happy as she missed the company. Her parents were strict but fair. Robert worked in the building trade and was lucky enough to have stable employment as a property repairer, having made many loyal customers. Hannah Mary prided herself on running a tidy house and everyone lived close by including Annie's grandparents, Auntie Priscilla, and Mike, the Scottie dog. Annie adored her grandmother and would sit with her some evenings, perched on a high stool, combing her long thick hair. In keeping with a strict regime, Annie would help her mother with any housework needed and at times a little washing up, although they had a cleaning maid most of the time. Meal times were a fairly quiet affair where elbows on the table were not tolerated. The absence of siblings to share such times made Annie's childhood happy but muted.

D.O.B. 22/09/1910

BURY

Bury was first mentioned as a parish in AD 962 and the name derives from an old English word meaning castle or fort. It is a town in Greater Manchester that lies on the River Irwell and emerged during the Industrial Revolution as a mill town centred on textile manufacture. The most imposing building in the town is Bury Castle, a medieval fortified manor house, built in 1469 by lord of the manor, Sir Thomas Pilkington, and was part of the house of York. In the mid 1800s the town started to grow when the factories, mines and foundries began to dominate the landscape. The textile industry and the domestic production of yarn and cloth greatly helped an unsettled economy and by the start of the twentieth century, the railways linking the neighbourhood mill towns and other industries such as paper making and calico printing thrived. Bury is also the regimental town of the Lancashire Fusiliers. In 1688, Prince William

Annie and the neighbourhood
children circa 1922.

Annie with mother, grandmother
and aunt circa 1921.

Bury Castle – Iron Age hill fort,
Exmoor, 2011.

of Orange landed in Brixham and with the help of some noblemen, raised regiments to help him oppose James II. Colonel Sir Robert Peyton raised a regiment containing six independent companies from the Exeter area and from July 1 1881, they became XX Lancashire Fusilliers, and have been involved in many vital campaigns such as the American War of Independence, the Napoleonic Wars, and both World Wars.

Annie went to an elementary Methodist school and then at the age of 11 she started at Eastward Council School. She was a bright eager child who took her 11 plus exam at the age of 10 and was a high achiever in Arithmetic, which she was taught by Mrs Beckett, a delicate woman with tiny hands and feet. She generally came top in needlework but found French a challenge. The children would sit five along a bench, an inkwell in front of each child and a fire blazing in a rough stone hearth. During summer, the windows would be thrown open wide to let the warm breeze in. The school day started at 9 and finished at 4. There was an hour for lunch and during winter, if there was brisk chill, you could take your sandwiches into the cellar. She was also taught household duties such as laundry and cookery and can remember making stewed apples and custard. The weekend was a time for play but attending Sunday school was compulsory, where bible studies and choir practice would be followed by going to her grandparents for tea, where a beautifully iced cake would sit on a china plate. Methodism was very strong in the mill towns of Yorkshire and Lancashire and the church would always remain vitally important to Annie. Later in life, she would become a Sunday school teacher herself.

At the age of 14 Annie left school and started a seven year tailoring apprenticeship with Richard Arnott, a well respected tailor in town. The reputation of a good tailor was very important in those days as it was not possible to walk into a shop and buy clothes off the peg. If you wanted a career as a tailor, you had to follow in the footsteps of a master craftsman and become a protégé. The system of apprenticeship was first developed in the Middle Ages and usually started in early teenage years, the apprentice living in the mentor's house and completing a legal contract. Annie remained at home though working a 47 hour week and her starting salary was five shillings a week. She worked in a small humid room above a shop in Bury and gave her mother most of her salary for her board. It was a long walk to work so when she was 19, her parents bought a Morris Oxford. As there were no driving schools and it was not required to pass a test, she was taught to drive by a family friend. With her new independence, Annie would take her parents for long drives into the Lancashire hills, enjoying quality time with them.

During the early Thirties, she was part of a group of friends who enjoyed dancing, going to the cinema, cycling and larking around. One day she met a boy called Samuel and he was a year older, tall and fair and he lived in the neighbouring town of Tottingdon. At that time they were both working in the cloth industry. Samuel worked for a firm of bleachers and dyers, a job that would stop soon as the war would bring a halt to all foreign trade. They married in 1936 when Annie was 25, considered old by some in those days. Annie wore a little pale blue dress with a lace collar and Samuel had a buttonhole with fresh flowers. They had their reception in the local Methodist church with at least 100 guests turning up from both sides of the family and Uncle Don, who managed the local Co-op store, organised the catering and laid out a spread of cold meats, pickles, onion tarts and dark nutty fruit cakes. Samuel took on a joint mortgage with his parents and they were able to move to a little semi detached house in Tottingdon and as the end of the Thirties approached, Annie and Samuel settled into the warm glow of their new life.

Before war broke out Samuel had been a cadet supervisor with the Sea Cadets so in 1940 he joined the Royal Navy and was posted overseas. Over the next four years, Annie would see very little of him but remembers being terribly proud of him when he came home, smart in his pressed naval uniform. It would prove to be a hard and lonely time but Annie continued working as a tailoress, staying with her parents regularly and making the best of things. She remembered the shortages and there not being enough margarine so you would have to use dripping on your sandwiches, always wrapping them in a damp cloth to keep them moist. They would all muck in together to get things done. Annie can remember neighbours in Wellington boots, spades in hand, digging back gardens for a vegetable patch as Violet May, the neighbour's daughter, skipped by on her way to school, clutching a Donald Duck gas mask in a little square box. Sometimes Annie would go to the pictures with some friends, usually before six as the queues weren't very long. They would grab the cheap seats at the front and watch the main film or maybe a B film but always the Pathe News. These little routines kept Annie mindful of the realities that faced her and helped her keep her spirits high.

The tide was going to change in 1944 as Samuel returned home from the war. Just having him back, there in her house, stretched out on the brown leather sofa by the window, made her feel happy. There was a lovely comfortable feeling as they went across the backyard and into the light and warmth of the kitchen. Early the following year, Annie gave birth to her first child, Christine. This was a blessing for the happy couple as Annie had previously had several miscarriages and was unsure whether she would ever carry a baby full term. When she fell pregnant with Christine she was encouraged to take to her bed regularly to rest, which Annie was quite happy to do if it meant her baby would survive. During the birth, Samuel waited anxiously behind the bedroom door until eventually he was handed his baby daughter. Sadly as much as Annie wanted to breast feed, the baby wouldn't take the milk so she grudgingly used the bottle, even under a table once as bombs dropped close by. There was an Anderson shelter in the back garden and they would sit in the dark, waiting for the all clear, listening to the creak of Aunt Priscilla's leather coat. The dim glow of evening would await them as they emerged, the street light blinking weakly. By the time Annie's second child came along, it would be a lot less dangerous. The end of the war was celebrated with street parties throughout the country, 'welcome home' banners and bunting strung up across roads, Union Jacks hoisted and trestle tables piled high with potted meat sandwiches, jelly and iced buns. There was a feeling of togetherness that had been absent before the war.

After the war Samuel was offered his old job back. Annie had by now given up her career, focusing instead on being a wife and mother, which was a full time job. In 1947, she gave birth to her second child, Susan. After a few years Samuel realised that he needed a change of direction and having lived in Lancashire all their lives, a new location felt quite exciting. They had enjoyed a holiday with the girls in Somerset a couple of years before so when they discovered a post office and general stores for sale in the area, they were curious. The decision was made when they discovered that east of the village lay an Iron Age hill fort called Bury Castle. The post office was

Annie in her late teens.

Porlock Post office today.

The church of St Dubricius.

in the pretty village of Porlock, which nestled in a deep lush hollow, surrounded by the hills of Exmoor and dense wooded valleys. It was heady and romantic and they jumped at the chance. It was 1953 and the country was just starting to get straight again.

POSTAL SERVICE

The postal story starts in the twelfth century when King Henry I appointed messengers to carry letters for the Government with private households making their own arrangements. Improvements were made over the next three to four hundred years with Henry III providing uniforms and Edward I creating posting houses. In 1516, Henry VIII created the Royal Mail, which would have to wait until 1635 to be available to the public, with a regular system of post roads, houses and staff. In 1661, Henry Bishop became the first Postmaster General, who introduced the Bishop Mark, a small circle with the month and the day inside. These were the first handstruck postage stamps. It was most common for the recipient to pay the postage until the postal reforms came in and on May 6th 1840, the Penny Black was introduced. The Victorians experimented greatly, from perforations to embossing and surface printing. The stamps of the 1860s and 1870s used the same profile of Queen Victoria but there was a variety of frames, watermarks and corner lettering. With the succession of Edward VII, new stamps became necessary but remained conservative until the innovations of King George V when a ¾ portrait was used for the first time.

It was the biggest sub post office outside of Minehead and would keep Annie and Samuel busy, occupying most of their time. The days were long and tiring as Samuel would work for twelve hours, starting at six in the morning, sorting mail out for the surrounding area. There were no first and second class stamps, just local and national and postcodes had yet to be created. Samuel would also deliver telegrams all over the countryside. It was a joint venture, with Annie working behind the counter, serving customers and also running the wool shop next door. They had a small thatched cottage that came with the shop, complete with an inglenook fireplace and old green Rayburn in the kitchen. The girls made new friends at the local school, which was just a short walk past St Dubricius' church, dating back to the thirteenth century, with its slate roof and coped verges. Even in those days Porlock attracted visitors due to its quaint look. It was nestled in some picturesque walking country and the family enjoyed visiting the tiny church at Culbone on a Sunday before going home for buttery baked apples with raisins stuck in where the cores had been. It was a close knit community and Alice was happy being a part of it for the next ten years.

In 1963, the family decided to sell the post office and move to Hill View Road in Minehead, a nearby coastal town with a tree lined promenade and streets of tall Edwardian houses. Samuel became one of the postmasters at a local post office and Annie started to teach needlework part time at the local community school. In her spare time, she proudly tended her garden. She also enjoyed cooking especially crumbly Genoa cakes for friends and shepherds pie, fish poached in parsley speckled milk, and bacon and eggs on a Sunday for the family. By this time, Christine had left home and was working in a post office in Burnham. Susan was now a teenager, still living at home and keen to earn her own living. The previous year she had started working as a chalet maid at Butlins holiday camp, becoming friends with one of the redcoats called Valerie. It was in

1964, whilst working at Periton Mead, a residential home surrounded by forest, that she was lucky enough to see the Beatles when they came to Minehead railway station, filming scenes for their first film, *A Hard Day's Night*. The calm of the station was shattered by the screams of hundreds of schoolchildren as a large crowd of excited teenagers gathered by the railway tracks. Their imminent visit had been plastered over the local papers the week before and Susan had arranged to finish work early. It was a Tuesday and she had enough money for an orange crush and a packet of No 6. She would get her wages on Thursday and give her keep to Annie, put a little in the bank and spend the rest on cigarettes.

In 1969, Samuel felt the time was right to retire and as both the girls had now left home, there were no ties. They had always had a love of Cornwall, its stunning coastline and variety of landscapes. Feeling confident about making another fresh move, they discovered a perfect little bungalow just outside of Truro and sold up. The dream would soon be cruelly dashed.

View from North Hill, Minehead.

The next few years would prove to be quite a challenge, with life dealing one devastating blow after another. Soon after moving to Cornwall, Samuel became very ill and whilst Annie tried her best to nurse him at home, he was eventually moved to a local hospital where he sadly died. Left reeling from the death of her husband, Annie attempted to rebuild her life, only to have to face an even more crushing trauma when her daughter Christine was diagnosed with Leukaemia. Despite all efforts to treat her, she died at the age of 39. Even though her life had been torn apart, she had to paste over the cracks for the sake of her grandchildren and made a decision to move to London temporarily to look after them. Soon after her son in law decided to take early retirement and became a full time father for the children. Eventually the time would come for Annie to move back to Cornwall to a cold house, breathing memories. She would feel more alone than ever.

West Somerset Railway, Minehead, 2011.

By now Annie was in her early seventies, and decided she would move again. She moved to Agre Road in Truro and here she would settle for the next twenty years. Susan continued to live in Minehead and they would speak on the phone once a week, seeing each other as often as possible. Annie would fill her time tending her garden, growing fruit and vegetables which she would often make into chutneys, filling the shelves in her garage, whilst an array of windfall apples would be scattered over sheets of newspaper. She would bake jam and curd tarts and occasionally take the bus to Falmouth to look around the shops. The church was an important part of her life and she sang in the church choir and the Salvation Army ensemble, giving her a well needed social life. She made friends with Sadie Penhaligon, who she had once taught needlework. Sadie had a son called David. This bright young man was a liberal MP, who was particularly prominent and impressive in the 1983 election campaign and a popular candidate for party leader. David died early one morning in a car crash on an icy road, leaving Sadie reeling from the shock. The two women would help and support each other, spending long winter evenings together in one or other's house.

When Annie reached the benchmark age of eighty, a surprise party was held and many guests travelled down from Lancashire. After a time, Susan felt it irresponsible to let Annie remain alone in her house and so she arranged for her mother to move to Stone Mill, a warden-led home in Minehead. It was 2003. Whilst there, she made good friends with a lady called Evelyn who is now at Wyndham House, where Annie has also been for the past couple of years.

EDITH WILKINSON

'You should always try and do your best.'

EDITH WAS BORN on January 10th 1910 in the small village of Coxley which lies on the River Sheppey near the cathedral city of Wells. She had one brother, Jim, who she was very close to. Her father James worked at St Cuthbert's Paper Mill just outside Wells and he would cycle to work. The paper mill had been there since the 1700s and used pure clear waters from the River Axe that rose two miles upstream at the Wookey Hole caves. Her mother Sarah stayed at home doing the cooking, cleaning and washing. This was a tiring job as water had to be fetched from the well and heated in an old fashioned copper kettle and due to the price of coal they burnt newspapers and old rags in a furnace in the back kitchen. The kitchen had a stone floor and she would cook on an old three burner Florence oil stove with an oven on top. In the corner of the larder sat a meat safe, keeping the flies away. Edith slept in the attic bedroom and if she woke in the middle of the night she had to light her way to the toilet with a candle as there was no electricity. If the wind blew the candle out it would give her a terrible shock. But they were luckier than most as a lot of houses still had outside toilets. The family lived in a row of cottages just on the edge of the village and on late summer afternoons Edith and Jim would often go and play around Fenny Castle (an old motte and bailey – motte is a mound and bailey is a courtyard – built around the twelfth century), with a bag of bruised apples to munch on.

Edith was very keen on school and was an eager and intelligent child, loving all sorts of lessons. The headmaster would set her little examinations and she and another equally bright boy would sit together because one of them was usually top of the class. The students sat in a big airy room with a high ceiling which had a roaring fire in the middle of the room during the winter. The fire had an ornate mesh guard around it and the younger students were in a separate room with radiators. Students used pencils when they were younger and then moved on to long tapered fountain pens and inkwells filled with black ink.

Edith only attended one school and was taught a variety of lessons from reading, writing and arithmetic to needlework and drill (the term used for physical education). In the third and fourth standards she took needlework which she would enjoy throughout her life and often helped her mother make her pinafore dresses. If you excelled at something at school there were no specific prizes but marks out of ten and when students arrived for school a register would be called, with all attendances noted and praised if regular. Edith lived locally so she would rarely be late and

D.O.B. 10/01/1910

Edie's brother Jim aged 15.

would go home to have lunch with her family. Most pupils walked to school in all weathers although some of the local farmers' children were taken by horse and cart which could be hired for three and sixpence. At the age of 11, Edith walked to Wells with the other girls to take Home Economics in a large Edwardian building with a grey slate roof. The boys would stay behind and take gardening.

Edith attended a Church of England Sunday school and sat at the back as she was quite shy. Going on outings with the church was a highlight of her life especially trips to Burnham or Weston on a horse and wagon with straw spread all over the wooden floor and the sun shining off the brasses on the bridle. The wagon would be packed with all the children, big and small, and some of the adults wore wide brimmed hats. The wagon would pull up outside the Royal Clarence Hotel and as everyone got off the pastor would give a coin to each child for sweets or a fruit bun. These are happy memories for Edith and the church would always play a big part in her life.

SUNDAY SCHOOLS

The first Sunday school opened in 1751 in St Mary's church, Nottingham. However the founding of these religious schools is more associated with Robert Raikes, philanthropist and Anglican layman, who saw the need to prevent children in the slums descending into crime. He initiated the Sunday school movement which began in 1780 in the home of Mrs Meredith. Initially only boys could attend but before long girls were to join. By 1831 Sunday Schools in Great Britain were attended weekly by over a million children and provided basic literary education alongside religious instruction. Most classes would take the form of a bible study session lasting for an hour or more and this would normally occur before, during or after a church service. Traditional children's hymns such as *The Wise Man Built His House Upon A Rock* and *Jesus Bids Us Shine* were often sung. In 1986 a new kind of Sunday school started in Brooklyn, New York called Sidewalk Sunday School in which the sermons were taken to project areas and parks and performed on little stages on the back of delivery trucks.

BURNHAM ON SEA

Burnham is a town on the edge of the Somerset levels, located at the mouth of the River Parrett. It started life as a small village and in the late eighteenth century it began to grow due to its popularity as a seaside resort. The history of Burnham has been dominated by sea defences since Roman times and in 1607 the Bristol Channel floods (supposedly caused by a tsunami) occurred when a tidal wave broke over the sea and 30 villages were deluged by water. The town is now defended from flooding by a large curved concrete wall that serves as a canvas for a variety of street art. There have also been many shipwrecks on the Gore Sands which lie just offshore.

Land at Burnham is mentioned as early as the late ninth century when it is mentioned in King Alfred's will as a royal domain and the name of the old settlement of Huish comes from 'hiwisc' which signifies a Saxon farmstead. Burnham and Highbridge were in the same parish

Edie's parents, James and Sarah.

and the church at Burnham was given to Gloucester Abbey in the twelfth century. At the end of the eighteenth century, Burnham saw the first phase of new growth as more traders started to congregate and a cattle market was started in 1797 as a result of the changes in farming practices. This would make Burnham more accessible and less off the beaten track. The railways accelerated the growth of both towns proving crucial to the nineteenth century expansion of Burnham as a holiday resort, as did the arrival of the grand Royal Clarence, the first hotel to be erected. Although the heyday of British seaside towns has passed Burnham has profited from improved communications and is now a popular commuter town.

When Edith left school she went to work at the Wiltshire Dairy. Most of the milk produced by dairy cows in Somerset was made into butter or cheese and often sent by rail to dairies in big towns or sold locally. The dairy was spotlessly clean and Edith remembers it being a very hard and busy job. She worked long days, setting off early from home for an 8am start and finishing at 6 in the evening, earning tuppence ha'penny an hour. During the summer most farms made Cheddar cheese as the cows were eating grass and in the winter Caerphilly cheese when they were eating hay. Her job was to pack six small chunks of cheese to a box or a withy basket and they were all individually wrapped in foil. She stacked these neatly in large containers ready for the local shops or the Nestle milk train that was going to Highbridge Market or Chippenham. Edith would work at the dairy until just before the war.

The close-knit community within the village of Coxley was an important part of Edith's life and there were many ways for friends to socialise. The church played a great part in the social scene as did friendly societies, fairs and local dances. Edith and a friend would go to a dance in Wells every Saturday night and they would walk the two miles home in the dark as there didn't seem to be anything to fear in those days. There would usually be a live band and her favourite dance was the Veleta, a ballroom waltz played out in triple time.

THE VELETA WALTZ

'Round dances' were couple dances where the dancers travelled around the ballroom instead of being fixed in one place. The other group within the Round Dances category were the simple sequence dances that followed a combination of steps in a pattern and included the *Schottische*, *Polka Mazurka*, *Varsoviana* and the *Two Step*. In the late 1800s the British Association of Teachers of Dancing started to run annual competitions to discover new sequence dances. These would be called *Old Time* or *New Vogue* dances and thus was born the 'choreographed' dance. Although other quadrilles such as the *Hussars* (1894) and the *Gordons' Square* (1898) were invented, the *Veleta Waltz* was seen as the first choreographed sequence dance although it didn't win a place the first time around. In 1900 the *Veleta* was revamped and soon became a ballroom favourite.

After working at the dairy for 14 years Edith went to work as a cleaning maid at Wells Cathedral School, where she worked during the war. It was one of the oldest independent schools in the country and Edith would enjoy the peace and quiet as she dusted the Vicar's Chapel,

Jim and Edie aged 8 and 10.

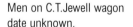

Men on C.T.Jewell wagon date unknown.

Coxley Church.

A family wedding in the Sixties.

The Pound Inn.

dragging her cloth up the stair rail as she climbed the stairs to the library. She would stare dreamily out of the window as the Claver Morris girls went past to class. Whilst there she became friends with another girl and it was only a matter of time before this friend introduced Edith to her cousin, Samuel. Britain was now in the aftermath of World War Two and Samuel, who had served overseas, had many stories to relate. When war broke out he was already in the Army and was then sent to serve in India. Edith's war had really been about working and taking care of her mother who was ill. Just after the war her mother died and Edith felt compelled to stay at home and look after her father, as her brother James had married and left home.

Samuel and Edith got married in Coxley Church in 1947 and moved into the family home. Edith's parents James and Sarah had always rented their cottage and the initials F.G. could be found chiselled on the brickwork by the landlord as a record of ownership. Edith and Samuel would eventually find a way of buying the cottage and they lived there all their lives.

Although work was fairly sparse Samuel found a job as a labourer. The following year Edith gave up work as she became pregnant. There appeared to be little professional help before or after giving birth although most friends rallied around in the village. As there were no ambulances, a friend took her to Wells Cottage Hospital where she was very well looked after. Edith started having contractions in the early hours of the morning and had a reasonably short labour, giving birth to William at 6.30 in the evening. Although she was unable to breast feed her baby through lack of milk, this far from prevented her forming a close bond with her son.

Edith and Samuel led a simple but happy life in Coxley. William was a quiet studious boy with a wide smile for everyone he knew. If it was the last Thursday in October, Edith would take William out for Punkie night, a Somerset version of Halloween, and they would parade through the streets carrying punkie lanterns carved from large orange skinned wurzels. It would make for quite a ghostly scene.

William grew up to be a stonemason, a highly skilled craft of shaping rough pieces of rock into accurate shapes and then arranging the stones to form a structure. He had served a long apprenticeship learning many of the traditional methods and when he was qualified he found work at Wells Cathedral. For a time William lived at home and Edith would send him off to work with his chisel and mallet wrapped in some sacking, a flask of coffee and smoked ham sandwiches.

WELLS CATHEDRAL

A Church of England cathedral and seat of the Bishop of Bath and Wells, Wells Cathedral is one of the most breathtaking and poetic of all the English cathedrals. It was built on the site of a late Roman mausoleum and the first church to be built there was established in 705 by King Ine of Wessex during whose reign the West Saxons started to mint coins. The Wells Cathedral that we see today was built between 1175 and 1490 and Bishop Jocelyn of Wells was responsible for its construction. Most of its structure is in the Early English style.

The cathedral has undergone many changes since the early days, from the Dissolution of the Monasteries in 1541 when income was reduced to the Monmouth Rebellion of 1685 when puritan soldiers caused much damage. During the Civil War many of the windows were smashed by soldiers although two of the oldest (dating back to 1280) have survived, on the west side of the Chapter House staircase. The Lady Chapel range dates back to 1325 and includes images of local Saint Dunstan who was an Abbot of Glastonbury Abbey and helped reform the English Church. Wells Cathedral now contains the most substantial collection of medieval stained glass in England.

Following a period of gentle decline a major restoration programme was needed by the middle of the 1800s and in the 1840s 'the great scrape' was initiated in which the whitewash was removed along with most of the medieval paint. The wooden galleries were removed and new stalls with stone canopies were placed further back with the line of the arches. It featured in the film *The Golden Age* about the reign of Queen Elizabeth I and a recent episode of *Doctor Who*. Perhaps the greatest celebration was held in July 2009 when Wells Cathedral hosted the funeral of Harry Patch, the last British Army veteran of World War 1, who had died at the grand age of 111 after spending his last years at Fletcher House in Wells.

Edie in her sixties outside her cottage in Coxley.

Edith and her son were incredibly close and when William wasn't working they would spend all their time together. She continued to love dancing and she and Samuel made up a foursome with her great friend Hilda Haskins and her husband, and they would go into Wells or Glastonbury on a Thursday evening. Edith remained very close to her brother Jim and his wife Sybil and sometimes on a Sunday the family would go and have a roast at The Pound Inn, but only if they had local lamb and mint sauce on the menu.

Edith often went on coach trips with her girlfriends, making sure they had permission from their husbands first. She remembers fondly a trip to Holland in the Sixties with her son which was unusual as holidays were often spent at her aunt's in Gloucestershire, doing ordinary things. She never wanted to do anything particularly exotic and was happy with the way things were.

The most important people in Edith's life were her husband, and son and so to lose them was far too painful to imagine. William passed away just before his father who died in the late Nineties. The memory of them both is sometimes far too much to bear. She has been at Fletcher House now for two years and has made some new friends, along with her old friend Hilda who is also at the home. She enjoys a good chat and always having something to knit. There is nothing she likes more than the smell of beef roasting in the oven but if you were to put a slice of beetroot on her salad, she'd have something to say. Edith thoroughly enjoys the variety of activities that Fletcher House organises especially drawing and painting and a nice landscape with rolling hills and a blue sky is her favourite sort of picture. The warmth and company she receives from all the caring staff at Fletcher House enables her to have a rich and happy life, making the future less daunting.

IVY SPRINGHAM

'I was determined to make the most of my life!'

IVY WAS BORN on October 6th 1910 to Arthur Thirgood and Emily Gold who lived at No 6 Victoria Road, Stanford Le Hope. Ivy's father was a blacksmith, a job which was a reserve occupation during the war and was quite well paid so the family were well provided for. Ivy's mother Emily was in service before she married and had worked as a cook and housekeeper. Ivy was one of three girls although her five year old sister Gertie died of diphtheria when Ivy was three. Her sister Emily was two years older and the girls got on well although Ivy was terribly spoilt as she was the youngest (her grandfather often gave her a piece of cheese if she didn't like her vegetables). Sometimes on the way to school Ivy waved to her grandma who would be sitting on the pavement outside her house crocheting a bedspread. Her granddad had left the quarry to work at Thames Haven before she was born and most of them lived on Brooke Road. The Golds were a very close knit family.

When Ivy was four the family decided to move further down the East Coast, as she had some chest problems and it was thought that the bracing air would help. Visits from the doctor were expensive, costing half a crown every time the doctor was called out, so it was advisable to stay healthy! The family moved to a street of a dozen houses within Shell Haven which was surrounded by oil tanks, refineries, ammunition factories and small petrol companies. During the war Tilbury Docks was a target and the girls were scared stiff to go in amongst all the tanks full of flammable petrol and oil, which they had to do occasionally to take lunch to their father who worked at one of the depots on site. As it was quite remote it was the responsibility of Shell Haven to arrange transport for employees and tenants as it was a six-mile walk to the nearest shops or to Fobbing church on a Sunday.

D.O.B. 06/10/1910

SHELL HAVEN
Shell Haven is a port on the north bank of the Thames Estuary and for over 80 years was the site of a large Shell oil refinery. In 1895 the ammunition firm Kynochs purchased Borley Farm to the east of Shell Haven Creek in order to open an explosives factory, which opened in 1897. The company was taken over by coal merchants Cory Brothers from Cardiff in order to build a storage depot which eventually became Coryton Refinery. The Shell Oil Company first arrived in the form of the Asiatic Petroleum Company in 1912 and they obtained a license to

Ivy (nearest the camera) aged 5 at Fobbing school, Essex.

Woody, Percy and Harold Gillett during a production by the Justhan's Amateur Dramatic society outside Bridge Road School, Grays, 1931.

store petroleum at Shell Haven in iron tanks each containing no more than 4,000 tonnes. Over the next thirteen years the site would also be the home of a distillation plant that produced fuel oil for the Admiralty and a manufacturing plant that made Bitumen for road surfaces. During WW2 the refineries and oil storage tanks at Thames Haven, Shell Haven and Coryton became a sitting target for air raids, notably in September 1940 during the Battle of Britain. The Shell refinery closed in 1999.

One of Ivy's earliest memories is of her fox terrier Judy following a sentry guard who was stationed outside her front door, patrolling the main gates. Ivy's mother took in lodgers as there were no hotels or guest houses for the employees or visitors to Shell Haven,. This was a friendly environment for early childhood and all the children from the cottages played together. At the end of the road was a big creek with fields on either side and Ivy can remember being happiest when she was playing with wooden hoops and mucking about with her best friend Joan Dowsett, Joan's brother Ron and Ivy's cousin Woody. They crossed wooden plank bridges over ditches and pulled chickweed out of the hedges to feed to her pet rabbits. Ivy also remembers playing with Ron on Meeson's Lane and throwing mud pies at the front doors until somebody called the local policeman.

Ivy went to Quarry Hill school which was a long low building with tiered slate roof. Lessons were taught in one large room and the elder and younger children were divided by a wooden panel. On cold days a small pot-bellied stove glowed in the corner, logs piled high in a basket. There was just one master who took the standards but he eventually left as he received his papers for war and was replaced by one of the women teachers.

When Ivy was fourteen she left school and her Aunt Jessie found her a job as a dressmaker's apprentice in London. The ladies of the Thirgood family had been wearing the well-tailored dresses for many years so when Ivy expressed an interest in dressmaking, Emily made enquiries. She had always been keen on sewing and had a Singer sewing machine on which she made the children's clothes whilst Arthur knitted the vests and swimsuits. So Ivy left the family home for the bright lights of London and although she didn't stay long she made the most of her time there. She had always enjoyed a stage show and for a special treat she was taken to see *Rose Marie* at the Drury Lane Theatre which opened in 1925 and ran for two years. It was London's most successful Broadway show after World War I and introduced a young aspiring American singer called Edith Day.

Soon after leaving London, Ivy enrolled herself on another apprenticeship in Westcliffe. This wasn't to last for long as her mother needed extra help with the lodgers following an accident. As there were no shops nearby food would be delivered from the village shop in Fobbing, and if you wanted fresh meat you had to place an order a week in advance with the butcher in Stanford Le Hope. This wasn't always necessary though as Grandad Gold kept rabbits, chickens and ducks and Arthur grew all the vegetables on his allotment. There was a certain regularity to the weekly menu. A roast on Sunday was followed by cold meat on Monday, shepherds pie on Tuesday, stew on Wednesday and fresh fish on a Friday, which would be delivered by a small van that came from Leigh on Sea. For a short while Ivy's teens were the picture of domesticity as she started heating water in the copper kettle at 6 am, scrubbed clothes against the washboard that leant against the kitchen wall and negotiated the three pronged dolly. She was the perfect wife in

Far left: Ron and Joan Dowsett playing tennis at Shell Haven, 1929.

Left: Percy's brother Albert and wife Doris, 1932.

waiting when she eventually met the boy she'd marry.

Ivy was 18 when she met Percy Springham. He was a mutual friend of her cousin and they met at a dance which had been organised to raise money for Justhan's, an amateur dramatic company to which Percy belonged. He was a natural entertainer and a great dancer and was showing off his Charleston moves when she first noticed him. Ivy found herself quite taken with this carefree lad and for the next few years they had a lot of fun together. They went to dances, played tennis, went on cycle rides and for long balmy walks. On Sunday afternoon Percy would call round and they would stroll across Orsett Heath to a public house called the Fox and Hounds where they enjoyed a shandy and a packet of crisps with salt in a little paper sachet, before wandering back through Hangman Woods where he would tell her tales of Dane holes. They married at St Mary's church in Little Thurrock on July 29th 1933 and spent their honeymoon in Eastbourne. They bought their first home in Grays with help from Percy's parents and settled into the warmth and calm of married life. They would live in this house all their lives. It wasn't long before two new challenges came along.

DANE HOLES

Letter of Feb 17 1706 from Dr Derham, the rector of Upminster …

' in Hangman's Woods is another hole of eighty foot and four inches. A cow fell into the hole but not killed and the carpenter went down and put ropes about her. The bottom is soft sand on which the cow alighted and was saved. The holes lie near the highway within the compass of six acres of ground leading from Stifford to Chadwell.'

A Dane hole is an underground structure consisting of a number of small chalk caves that can be entered by a vertical shaft. They are often seen as ancient chalk mines with the shaft blackened by smoke. Pliny the Elder writes that the Dane holes were being exploited during pre history and the word is derived from Anglo Saxon, meaning hole or valley. Henry III gave everyone the right to sink a marl pit on their own land as spreading chalk on the land was common practice in the Middle Ages. Local tradition insists they are readymade hiding places for smugglers or Northern invaders and may have been used by illicit traffic as they are difficult to approach and dangerous to descend.

Right: Eastbourne – Ivy with Doreen, 1938.

Far right: Dad and Ann in the garden (the corrugated iron roof on the chicken run used to be part of the Anderson shelter), 1950.

First holiday after the end of the war! Late July school holidays in Paignton, Devon, 1945.

In 1935 whilst doing the ironing Ivy went into labour and without too much pain and discomfort their first child Doreen was born. Just as Ivy was getting used to having a small baby Percy was taken very ill with peritonitis and was rushed into the London Hospital by ambulance. It took him nearly six months to recover so Ivy moved back to live with her family in Shell Haven as she needed the help and support of her family.

When the war started Percy was working as a bricklayer at Shell Haven redoing all the boilers and furnaces. The job was very dangerous and he had to crawl along wooden boards which were still warm and burning underneath him with a serious risk of them catching fire. He was also sent to Kings Lynn to help in the construction of an aircraft hangar and built housing for the RAF in Ellesmere Port which was a protected job and part of the war effort. Percy was also in the Home Guard and was lucky enough to have a proper rifle and not a wooden one. Ivy was extremely proud of her husband during this time and coped as best she could with a small daughter and all the dangers the war held. There was a shelter at the bottom of the garden made of corrugated iron and it had wooden seats, wire-framed bunks and Californian poppies that grew around the edges. Tilbury Docks were very close and Ivy could hear the sirens wail as planes were spotted crossing overhead or if there was a risk of flooding. She walked Doreen to school going through the gate at the bottom of the garden and along the edge of a field past tall poplar trees, watching as her daughter ran quickly through the school gates.

Just after the war Ivy gave birth to her second daughter Ann. Doreen had just started secondary school and Ivy remembers it being a severe winter, with the snow reaching the top of the fence. Percy still worked as a bricklayer for Shell Haven and it was now Ivy's job to look after her family which she did with great pleasure.

By the start of the 1950s the Springham family had settled into a happy routine. Ann had started at a local school and Doreen went to work in London for Sheen Accounting, organising the shipping and payroll ledgers. London was still greatly scarred by the Blitz and rubble was still being cleared. Doreen can remember seeing a fireplace, the only remnants of a family home, left on a wall, several floors up. On another occasion she watched out of the window at work as the Queen went by on the Royal Coach after King George had died. The rest of the family watched the procession on a next-door neighbour's black and white television, constantly trying to readjust the picture. Doreen was still living at home and paying Ivy £1.50 a week board and lodging.

When Percy had spare time he grew vegetables on his allotment which was still necessary due to ongoing food shortages. On Saturday evenings Granddad Springham would come over to the house with a bag of shrimps and the men would drink hot gin and tonic, heated by the poker from the fire. Ivy still enjoyed a walk across Orsett Heath on a Sunday evening and would stop at the Fox and Hounds just like she did when they were courting. In her spare time Ivy went to cake decorating classes in the afternoon and would take Ann to Bastiani's for ice cream after school. She was immensely house proud and adored housework, longing to show off her home, especially the embroidered fire screen she had made. She also loved her garden, especially the fish pond and the ornate stone bird bath that was used to cycle around when Anne was learning to ride her bicycle.

Ivy and Percy taking pride in their fish pond, 1949.

Far left: Clapton 1952

Left: Four generations! Emily Thirgood, Doreen holding baby Linda and Ivy outside Emily's thatched cottage in Grays, 1962.

Ivy at Ann's house
aged 82.

Ivy aged 80 with Alison,
Doreen, Emily and
Michael, the great
grandchildren.

Life in the 1950s was just about keeping your family nice as they recovered from the war.

Towards the end of the 1950s Doreen got married but sadly Percy had pneumonia and had to go straight to bed after the reception. Ivy continued to look after the family but looked forward to Wednesday afternoons when her great friends Mrs Garrod and Mrs Jeff would come and visit, and they would put the world to rights over a cup of tea and a slice of ginger cake. On Fridays she visited her mother on the bus, picking up the shopping on the way, but the weekends were always saved for Percy. These were her little routines and her life gave her all the satisfaction she needed.

Doreen had her first child Linda in 1962 and when the baby was just 3 months old the family had a lucky escape when they were involved in a road accident. Luckily seatbelts were still voluntary because if they had been wearing them it could have been much worse. Ivy suffered a black eye and the other passengers were stiff and bruised but Percy suffered some injuries and mild paralysis, which led him to being bedbound in hospital for some time with sandbags packed in either side. This was one of many ailments that Ivy nursed him through.

In 1967 Ann turned 20 and married Graham in St John's church in Grays. Ivy helped them to move by piling their belongings into a wheelbarrow and pushing it just six houses along the street. The next few years would be austere as Britain struggled through an uncertain time of strikes, mass unemployment and industrial unrest. Ann and Graham were still renting their home as it was fairly difficult to get a mortgage especially during the '3 day week'. Graham would dig drains and collect wood from the rivers to make extra money. Although times were hard, the whole country came together.

THREE DAY WEEK

In the early 1970s there were incredibly high rates of inflation which caused unrest in many trade unions, especially in the mining community. The 'three day week' was one of several measures introduced in Britain by the Conservative Government to conserve electricity as production was limited due to industrial action by the coal miners. From 1st January to 7th March 1974 the working week was cut to three days consumption of electricity for commercial use and a ban on overtime. Television stations stopped broadcasting at 10 pm to conserve electricity and by the end of January there were nearly 3 million people unemployed. The miners strike began in February but was brought to an end early in March following a Labour victory at the general election.

The family spent every August at the same hotel in Hastings run by a lady called Mrs Millicent. The rooms were clean and bright and the dining room was oak panelled with a cut glass decanter full of sherry and a silver tray of crystal glasses laid out on the sideboard. She served three meals a day and the food was usually very tasty except for the braised lamb which had been stewed for hours and tasted rather unpleasant. Every year they expected the sun to shine but it usually rained. The other occasion for everyone to be together was Christmas and the house would be so full that a couple of trestle tables were laid. There wasn't much money to buy presents so Percy made a swing and if they were lucky they received slippers or a dressing gown.

In the 1970s the thrill of European holidays beckoned. Ivy and Percy travelled to Austria and flew to Italy once, staying in a small pension in Florence with their old friends Bill and Peggy

Jarvis. They visited Rome and the Vatican City and once went on a package to Rimini. They also took another holiday to Switzerland with friends Rene and Sid, which was quite likely to have been the last time they saw him alive. Percy and Sid had been friends for some time and he occasionally helped out in Sid's menswear shop in Tilbury. One day Sid was alone in the shop and a gang of masked men wielding hammers descended upon the shop. Ivy comforted Rene when the horrors seemed too much and said silent thanks that Percy had not been in the shop that day.

The Silver Jubilee gave Britain cause to celebrate and Ivy remembers people making their own flags and draping bunting around lamp posts, stringing it from one side of the street to the other. Children played games in the streets like 'walk the plank' and all the women cooked a mountain of food which was laid out on long tables covered with Union Jack paper cloths. Ivy was not able to enjoy the festivities much as Percy had again become ill and would pass away the following year.

Life without Percy was to prove exhausting and sad until she woke one day and thought 'I'm going to paint these walls a fresh new colour'. Ivy was now in her seventies and determined to make the most of her life. She found a new lease of life and a trusted companion in her old friend Mrs Garred, whom she had known since the 1930s. They would support each other through the next few years and when Mrs Garred died unexpectedly it was Ivy who found her, slumped against the kitchen door. Ann comforted her mum that evening as they raised a glass of brandy to her memory.

Ivy celebrated her 90th birthday with all the family around her and even joined in the games. The grandchildren had a collapsible tunnel that they persuaded Ivy to crawl through on her hands and knees and pushing and pulling they managed to get her out the other end. In 2007 Ivy went on holiday to stay with Doreen in Somerset and never went back. Now there are more people in Ivy's life than ever before. She has moved to Greenhill Residential home and has a new best friend in a lady called Betty. When Ivy looks at the photographs from her 100th birthday party she sees all the people who care and her spirits soar.

Doreen, Ivy, Gillian and Aaran, mid Nineties.

IRENE HARDWICK

'I lived in a mobile home for almost half a century!'

IRENE WAS BORN in Goole, Yorkshire on 19th October 1906 and had two brothers, Jim and Eric. When Irene was 14 her mother gave birth to another girl called Mary who now lives in Canada. Her father Ben Abson was a seaman who sailed out of the London Docks on the *Lord Richey* and if the children behaved he would take them out on his boat. Irene's mother Jeanette was delicate and liked a glass of port but she did her best for all the children and when she was sober she had a job working as a cook at the Station Hotel. Things did not always go smoothly if Jeanette was drunk and Irene can remember many Christmas days when she had to fill her brothers' stockings and help prepare the meal. Everything felt better in the evening when they sat around the piano and Ben would play *Roses are blooming in Picardy*, one of Irene's favourite songs. A very popular song at the time, it was sung by British soldiers who had left a sweetheart behind on their way to fight on the Front at Flanders.

GOOLE – A YORKSHIRE TOWN

Goole is a port town where the River Don and River Ouse merge, in the East Riding district of Yorkshire. Goole is a very significant inland port and it has extensive dockyards. Coal is the most dominant commodity handled although textiles, ship repairs and sugar refining are also leading industries. Goole also has a regular cargo liner service to many places in Europe, and North and South Africa. It was once a small village that made its living from draining the marshes when in 1626 the Dutch civil engineer Cornelius Vermuyden diverted the River Don northward to the River Ouse to drain the marshland, at the request of King Charles I. Goole is the nexus of a network of villages such as Hook, Airmyn, Swinefleet and Rawcliffe. Its industrial landscape is visible from a distance and its most prominent landmarks are the twin water towers dubbed the 'salt and pepper' pots.

The family lived at one of the smaller houses on Fourth Avenue and when Irene was older they all moved to a bigger house across the road, which had two bedrooms and an attic room upstairs, and three large rooms downstairs. Everyone knew each other on Fourth Avenue. The corner shop was owned and run by the Woffenden sisters and along the outside wall was a fine display of wooden crates full of apples, tomatoes, frilly lettuces and bunches of radishes. The

D.O.B. 19/10/1906

Irene with her mother and brothers Jim and Eric, early 1910s.

Grandad Holland, Edna, little Trevor and Irene on a trip to Bridlington, early 1940s.

sisters were well known for wearing men's clothing and an 'icky thump' cap back to front, which caused quite a stir at times. They were nicknamed Tip and Tep and Irene remembered one winter evening Tip was hiding under the back stairs with a keg of beer in her lap and a rolled up cigarette hanging out of her mouth, hiding from her husband. Her father kept striking matches for her but she would just blow them out and push him away.

Irene went to Alexander Street School which was a mile away and she had to cross a main road, go under a railway bridge and through a subway to get there. Irene always felt quite safe in Goole and often took her brothers to school as well as running errands for local workers, delivering lunches for tuppence. Irene enjoyed arithmetic and was an avid reader, often visiting the library on Carlisle Street. She also loved to play the piano and her piano teacher Miss Mary Oxley was always very encouraging. However this was to change when her sister Mary was born as Irene would have to give up playing, as the family could not afford to continue with the lessons. Miss Hibbetson and young Miss Precious, two of Irene's favourite teachers, were very good friends and would often go for a drink at the Airmyn Arms in town. Irene regularly attended Sunday school and followed the Catholic faith until she decided to join the Church of England when she was 16. She felt that the catholic priests were not setting a good example and recalls that 'they would come on a Saturday often drunk and you would have to have your half crown ready, which you paid for the sermon, and Father Turkin would put a mark on your little red card'. She never returned to the Catholic faith.

When Irene was 12 towards the end of World War I she was out of town with her brothers when a succession of bombing raids took place - the Zeppelins were attempting to bomb the docks. Goole is one of the largest inland ports and would have been considered a target. Many people took shelter under a haystack in Airmyn and Irene distinctly remembers a large girl called Minnie who smelt rather unpleasant and constantly pulled a large brown comb through her thick hair.

Irene left school at 14 to look after her mother, who was suffering from tuberculosis, as her father was still away at sea. She would take charge of all the domestic chores, filling the brick furnace with cardboard from the shop next door and boiling water in large copper pots. Coal was delivered on a horse and cart and an acquaintance called 'Mad Harry' from Hook would come with a churn of milk on a horse and trap. When her father was home he gave her money to go and buy beef skirt from the butchers on Pasture Road and they would have a meat and potato pie on a Thursday and rabbit once a week, as it was very cheap. Certain foods were still rationed so you had to make ends meet.

When Irene was 22 she moved to Shipley and for the next seven years worked in service for the Ramsey family where she did mainly domestic chores, cooking and acting as a nanny for one of the younger children. The eldest daughter Rose was a childhood friend from Goole who was sadly lost at the age of 22 after an illness. This was a sad time for Irene. After leaving Shipley, Irene moved back to Goole and after visiting the labour exchange found work in a butcher's shop making pork pies. She earned 9 shillings a week, most of which she would give to her mother. Irene was very assertive when necessary so when she was expected to clean soiled nappies by the butchers wife she refused, and her employment was terminated. Irene's mother finally passed away when Irene was 28 and although her father was heartbroken she felt an enormous amount of relief.

The Pasture Public Baths in Goole were innovative and a place to meet friends and socialise. In winter the owners fitted a skating rink and at other times of the year they placed a false floor over it and held a dance once a month, which cost a shilling and gave the local bands a chance to play to a willing audience. One Saturday night Irene went with a few friends wearing a very pretty frock, and struck gold. She married Ken in 1937 in the local parish church and they had a little reception at home. They rented their first home on Pasture Road from a work colleague of Eric's and it cost them 15 shillings a week. Although he trained as a blacksmith Ken now had a job at a local paper mill that paid a reasonable salary, which was going to be helpful as their first child would soon arrive. Irene gave birth to Pete at home and a woman from Howden came and lived with the family to help out.

During the war Ken was in the Territorial Army and was stationed at Grimsby on the anti-aircraft guns which were there to protect the docks. Ken was stationed with a really good friend of Irene's, Edna Smith, who also lived on Fourth Avenue and knew the family. Irene's father Ben was still living with her and had a job as a watchman for the wheat stores aboard the *Archibald Russell* which was moored at the docks. Ken was away for long periods and would only come back with a 24-hour pass, and Jim and Eric were away in the army in Egypt, so Irene was alone with a small child. She remembers it being quite a scary time and she often woke up shaking at the sound of bombs in the distance. The Germans bombed the docks regularly and she would retreat to the shelter which was a thick brick construction with a concrete roof on top opposite the back door. The shelter in the garden remained for a few years after the war and was eventually knocked down in the 1950s. The schools had underground structures with sheets of tin over the top which were usually grassed over. There were no evacuees in Goole as children were not sent to any town or city which was under threat of aerial bombardment.

Irene and Edna in Bridlington, 1950s.

ANTI AIRCRAFT WARFARE

Mainly used for air and homeland defence, anti-aircraft warfare was a way of detecting hostile aircraft and destroying them. The maximum distance at which a gun or missile can engage an aircraft is an important figure. By the late Thirties the British definition was "that height at which a directly approaching target at 400 mph can be engaged for 20 seconds before the gun reaches 70 degrees elevation". Throughout the twentieth century air defence was one of the fastest evolving areas of military technology, responding to the evolution of aircraft. Air defence had included other elements during World War II such as searchlights to illuminate aircraft at night and tethered barrage balloons which were used to prevent aircraft flying below the height of the balloons, and also to act as a physical obstacle to bomber aircraft over cities.

In the aftermath of the war Britain gathered strength and rebuilt its shattered limbs. Every family had to pull together and food shortages continued into the 1950s. Pete and Trevor took their sweet coupons to Edna Holland's shop once a week, excitedly waiting for a handful of pear drops to be dropped in a paper bag until one day she said "I don't need your coupon as sweets have come off ration." The boys were giddy with sugar for the rest of the day.

Irene's marriage was unsettled after the war as Ken was partial to a drink and could be quite nasty at times. He continued working at the paper mill and Irene had part time cleaning jobs. She

Irene and her friend
Wendy, 1980s.

Irene and Trevor's wife Marjorie
at a traction steam rally at High
Ham near Langport, 1970s.

Irene and Trevor, 1970s.

had a cluster of good female friends for support, none more so than her best friend Edna Holland whom she had known since school days. Together they had memorable holidays to the seaside town of Bridlington, especially the time in 1949 when they took little Trevor and Grandad Holland, whose best accolade was the fact that he had built a fireplace with one hand.   These were happy times amidst a broken nation.

In 1958 Ken's job at Ferry Bridge power station came to an end and being a rigger he was offered a job at the new 'A' station being built at Hinkley Point in Somerset. The original Magnox reactor was being constructed and the power station would start generating electricity for the National Grid in 1965. At the height of the project Hinkley would employ 2,600 people and many would have come from northern towns. This was the start of a new life for Irene. The family made the move on the train leaving all their possessions behind and lived at The Shoulder of Mutton at Westonzoyland for two months. At this time they decided to rent a caravan at a site called Lakeside in Bridgwater where most of the tenants were employees of Hinkley Point. Trevor was thirteen and started at Blake College on the edge of town. As the option of buying a mobile home was so much cheaper than a house (they had no rates to pay and the ground rent was 75p a week) they decided to buy their own caravan. Irene would live at Lakeside for 49 years.

After the dark Northern terraces, moving down south was a blessing for Irene. Not only was Somerset idyllic but her relationship with Ken improved as he drank less and was generally much happier. Trevor and his dad would start to bond again, finding quiet rivers where they could cast their fishing rods and wait for a bite. When Trevor was 17 he decided to move back to Goole temporarily in order to help his brother Pete who was running a garage. Although the move was to prove fruitless commercially he did meet Marjorie and they returned to Somerset together, moving in with Irene and Ken. Although it was by now the early 1960s things were still fairly basic on the site. There was an outside communal toilet and no running water in the caravan, so tenants had to fill a bucket from the stand pipe. There were no telephones so calls had to be made from the telephone box and black and white television was still the rage. The one thing that was not lacking was community spirit. There is nothing but happy memories of those days at Lakeside and Irene had a lot of very good friends and neighbours. There were Mary and Jim Logan, a big friendly Scot who liked a tipple and would squeeze all the breath out of you when he gave you a hug, and Bill Chinn the butcher who was grumpy but good hearted and always made sure there was an extra chop in the bag. Irene will always remember these people with only the fondest of memories.

Irene never had a job and instead spent her days doing the things she enjoyed. She caught a little bus that came to Lakeside and would go blackberry picking, five days a week while the season lasted. Irene had now become very close to Marjorie and when she wasn't working in the motorcycle shop they would go on days out together to Taunton, Weston and Bristol especially Lewis' department store. Along with another great friend Lou Lou the girls advanced on all the big stores and caused mischief by trying on different hats and spraying clouds of perfume around. Sadly Lou Lou moved back to Birmingham to be with a cousin who had lost her husband and never returned.

Irene still travelled back to Goole fairly regularly to visit her son Pete and best friend Edna, but she never felt the need to return permanently. As she travelled home on the train and watched the roof tops and chimney stacks of the North disappear from view, she would look forward to getting back to Somerset. In 1968, the family pulled together to support Trevor and Marjorie, who lost a baby that was only 10 days old. Although they would never have another child, their love for each other has always kept them strong.

During the 1970s and 1980s the family were never far apart from each other. They went out together regularly as a foursome and if a night out was called for the family would descend on the Golden Bowl in Bridgwater for a steak and a bottle of Piat D'Or. In 1980 Marjorie bought a white Ford Fiesta and took the family on many outings. They had cream teas at the Old Mill at Uffculme and paid regular visits to their favourite pubs like the Plough at Holford, then went off to Dunster for a stroll to Gallox Bridge. The Crown at Catcott where Irene had her 75th birthday party was also a favourite, although Marjorie was furious when she found out that May the landlady had made a sponge instead of a fruit cake! Over the years the two women became incredibly close and Irene still treats Marjorie like a daughter.

Irene and Ken, 1980s.

Irene and Ken had enjoyed a good marriage since the move to Somerset. Ken stayed at Hinkley Point for many years and then found a job with British Cellophane. When he eventually retired Irene found he got under her feet and insisted on offering advice on housework. Trevor was now working as an engineer and during the 1980s he and Marjorie could afford to buy their own bungalow, which they still live in now. They made the move in the works' truck and Ken dug the garden over as they unloaded. The earth was already hard and the nights were drawing in. It was the beginning of December. Irene usually hosted Christmas but once Trevor and Marjorie moved to the bungalow the tables were turned. For the first time in many years Irene could sit back, pull a cracker and have the energy to enjoy the Christmas dance at the British Legion that she and Ken went to every year

Irene, Ken and Marjorie at Lakeside, 1980s.

It was a bolt from the blue for Irene when she lost her husband. The family had travelled up to visit Pete in Goole when one morning whilst having a shave Ken had a cerebral haemorrhage and died instantly. He had been singing along to the radio when it happened. It was all very sudden and a terrible shock for Irene, who had been waiting at the breakfast table for him.

Irene returned to Lakeside after a few days and her good friends on the caravan site Jean and Florence were there for her. She continued to live at Lakeside until a terrible gust of wind pulled her out of the caravan. She had her hand through an old dog collar that was attached to the door and this probably saved her as without it she would have fallen forward and cracked her head on the stone steps. It stripped the skin off two fingers but crucially saved her life. She spent 10 days in Musgrove Park Hospital and a further 7 weeks in Bridgwater Hospital and eventually social workers found her a place at Oak Trees residential home. Irene has been very happy in the home and her room has been transformed with all the mementos from her life, making it like her front room in the caravan. The best time of the day though is when she has a visit from Trevor and Marjorie, and they bring Charly the Jack Russell who curls up on her lap. This final touch of warmth and familiarity makes all the difference to her.

HILDA GROVE

'I did all the things that ladies do!'

D.O.B. 22/09/1909

A LITTLE FURTHER from Westminster and the River Thames, Edward III gave the manor of Kennington to his oldest son Edward 'the Black Prince' in 1337. The Prince built a large palace between Cardigan Street and Sancroft Street where Parliament met in 1340 and Chaucer was employed as Clerk of Works in 1389.

Born in Kennington on September 22nd 1909, Hilda grew up in a city on the brink of war. Her parents were Annie Agnes and Fredrick Crafter and she had a brother, Fred, and a younger sister, Doris. Her father was an electrician and worked for the local borough but times were fairly tough, and her mother stayed at home keeping a tidy house and managing the finances, at which she was very good. Hilda experienced frequent air attacks, as strategic bombing had its beginning during World War I when German Zeppelins and Gotha bombers started raiding London. By 1915 'squadron size' raids by numerous Zeppelins had begun and they were always at night, in the dark of the moon. This unsettled time was made equally difficult by fuel shortages, and vehicles were converted to run on coal gas. Because of the frequent air raids lighting restrictions were also imposed in 1916.

Whilst at school Hilda met the boy that she always described as the true love of her life. His name was Bill and no-one else ever compared. They were inseparable and did everything together. They rode their bicycles to Wimbledon Common on sunny Saturday afternoons and spent long hours engrossed in each other's company. Then one day Bill started to complain of a dry throat and developed a cough. Although they visited the doctor many times (which wasn't cheap in those days), it seemed that no peculiarities were detected. Bill became very sick and his mother and Hilda kept a vigil at his bedside until the moment he passed away. Hilda was seventeen when Bill died and the pain of losing him was immeasurable. These memories have stayed with her ever since and she has never forgotten him.

After leaving school Hilda went to work as a copy typist on the Tottenham Court Road. She remembers working in the typing pool, a strictly female arena, where the only time you might see a man at a typewriter was if he was an author. People came in if they wanted a letter, essay or a novel typed, so if you were exceptionally fast you got the best jobs. The writer Hillaire Belloc was a frequent visitor. Hilda was still living at home with her family and cycled to work through the streets of London. The weekend was a welcome relief from the busy week and she would often

Right: Doris, Fredrick and Hilda Crafter.

Far right: Hilda, 1930s.

Baby Hilda with brother Fred, 1911.

go with friends to see a film in the West End. It is quite likely the girls would have gone to see Alfred Hitchcock's *Blackmail* which was the first British sound feature film. The film began production as a silent movie until the studio decided to turn it into a 'talkie' during shooting, although they had to use another actress to dub the dialogue due to Anny Ondra, a popular actress of the time, having a thick Czech accent.

HILAIRE BELLOC

Born in 1870 near Paris in a small town called St Cloud, he spent most of his life in the South of England. He was by far one of the most prolific writers Britain has ever seen and his *Cautionary Tales* are probably the most widely known of his work along with numerous collections of poetry and essays. He was also a highly successful novelist, writing books such as *Mr Clutterbuck's Election* (1908) and *Pongo the Bull* (1910).

After serving in the French Army, he graduated from Balliol College, Oxford and had published *A Bad Child's Book of Beasts* and *Verses and Sonnets* by the time he was 26. He was a member of the Fabian Society and during his early career as a journalist he became great friends with George Bernard Shaw and H.G. Wells. After he traversed the political stage for a few years, becoming a Liberal candidate for South Salford and being elected to the House of Commons in 1906, he was tempted back to his one great love, writing, and returned to journalism. He wrote for many news sheets and periodicals and became editor of the popular political weekly *The Eye Witness* and also attacked the political establishment in his book *The Party System* (1911). He also exposed examples of political corruption including the involvement of David Lloyd George in the Marconi scandal.

Hilaire Belloc was a strong supporter of Britain's involvement in World War I and he helped the war effort whenever he could. He became military correspondent for *Land and Water*, a weekly periodical that dealt with the war, and made frequent visits to the Western Front. He told his readers that "the war was a clash between Pagan Barbarism and Christian Civilisation" and often exaggerated German casualities, saying "one should always lie in the interests of the nation". He lost many friends during the war including his son Louis Belloc who was in the Royal Flying Corps, and was killed while bombing a German transport column in August 1918. Asked once why he wrote so much he replied, " because my children are howling for pearls and caviar".

Hilda and Jack's wedding day, May 5th 1936.

The arrival of the 1930s brought an unexpected invitation for Hilda. She was good friends with a girl from work and one day the girl's brother invited Hilda to a dance. The boy was Jack Grove. After having a wonderful time they strolled home from the Palais, his arm around her shoulders. They courted for 6 years and Hilda often thinks this was too long and that it probably did not help their relationship. Although she may not have wanted to with Jack, she thinks people should live together before they get married as it gives them a chance to see if they are compatible.

Hilda and Jack married in 1936 at St Paul's church, Lorimar Square and they took a room in a small hotel in Boxhill for their wedding night. The thing about Jack Grove was that he grew on her. He was a very good-looking man and she was very proud to have him as a husband. Their first home was a three bedroomed house in Sanderstead, Surrey that backed on to the most beautiful bluebell wood. Jack had studied for a long time and was a successful chartered accountant with an office in Buckhurst Hill and he commuted by train to his office every day.

Just before the war in 1938, after an easy labour in a nursing home, Hilda gave birth to a beautiful baby girl and named her Ann. Hilda totally adored her baby daughter and she faced

Hilda and Jack enjoying early married life.

Hilda with Ann and Raymond
at Westgate, 1948.

Hilda, Jack with Raymond
and Anne, Brighton 1950s.

many unpredictable and difficult times protecting her from the dangers of war and especially the doodlebugs. The V1s made a terrible droning sound and as soon as the noise stopped, you had about 15 seconds to escape the powerful blast. They were fired from France when it was captured by Hitler and he targeted large swathes of South East England and London. After war broke out Hilda would spend long evenings as she sheltered under the stairs, keeping a watch on Ann who was tucked up in a cot, and feeling scared and worried for Jack who was out on Home Guard duty. Regardless of the dangers Hilda was still incredibly happy, as becoming a mother had given her the purpose and joy she so often felt may have been missing from her life.

In 1948, after a tricky labour, Hilda gave birth to her son Raymond and soon the family moved to a new home. The Dell was a sprawling house on the edge of Epping Forest with parquet flooring, solid beech and pale timber furniture, gleaming Pyrex glassware on the kitchen shelves and a beautiful terraced garden that Hilda enjoyed tending for many years.

For the next few years Hilda and Jack enjoyed their suburban life. Ann went to a boarding school in Bexhill and although she was initially very homesick, she would make many friends and enjoy her schooldays. When Raymond was 8, Jack encouraged Hilda to enrol their son at a boarding school in Birchington in Kent, even though Hilda felt her son was too young and would have preferred him to stay with her as they were incredibly close. Hilda was given the opportunity to visit Raymond whenever she wanted as Hilda's sister Doris and her husband Rodney had bought an end of terrace cottage in Birchington. Whenever Hilda visited they strolled along Minnis Bay which was surrounded by chalk cliffs and caves, or visited the beautiful ancient churchyard which was the final resting place of the Pre Raphaelite artist Dante Gabriel Rossetti. Often instead of shopping they had steak pie in front of the fire at the Railway Inn.

The sisters had always been very close and their sons, who had grown up together, were best friends. The two families had been spending holidays together for years. They had adjoining rooms in a little hotel at Westgate near Margate where the twin beds had impeccably tucked edges and they served tinned oranges for dessert. Hilda would send the men off for a vanilla cone and she and Doris would stroll barefoot in the sand or relax in a deckchair, paperback in hand as the boys built sandcastles. At Christmas time they alternated between spending Christmas Day at

Hilda's in Kent and Boxing Day at Doris' in Surrey, until to avoid all the travelling they decided to spend it at the Westcliffe Hotel in Bournemouth where the whole family spent the festive period.

In 1964 Hilda and Jack decided to separate. Although they had been happy enough it had never been a perfect relationship and Hilda freely admits to relishing her new life alone. She continued to live in the Dell with Raymond whilst Ann had finished a course at Secretarial College and had decided to go travelling to New Zealand where she stayed for 25 years. Hilda had never had a job since marrying as there was never any need to. She and the children were well provided for as Jack had a well paid job, and now as a single lady she could start to enjoy a life of leisure. One of Hilda's great passions was playing bridge, a 'trick taking' card game played by four players in two competing partnerships using a standard deck of 52 cards. To be good at this game you had to be a skilled tactician, have a good memory and communicate well. She was a member of a club and they played up to five afternoons a week and for many years the game and the social life it created became a big part of her life and made her very happy.

Christmas at the Westcliffe Tower Hotel, Bournemouth, 1959 (Doris, Johnny, Hilda and Raymond).

BRIDGE

The origin of playing cards lies in China where paper was invented, and can be dated to 1120. Originally cards were used for gambling and fortune telling and tarot cards were first introduced in Italy in 1440, although slightly earlier Saint Bernado had warned the 'Faithful' that cards were invented by the Devil and were often regarded as the 'Devil's Picture Book'. In 1495 Henry VII issued a decree forbidding his servants from playing cards except during the Christmas holiday. By this time suits had began to appear on cards and the first three suits were presumably adapted from German leaves, hearts and hawkbells.

Bridge was derived from Russian Whist, originally called Biritch, meaning a player can 'announce or herald' their auction. Books on Whist have been known to date back to the 1700s.

The English started to play Bridge in a 'duplicate' method in 1857, to try to eliminate most of the luck associated with the deal of the cards. Early accounts indicate that in 1903 some of the British civil servants stationed in India created a method of bidding the trump suit which was coined 'auction bridge'. Whilst on board ship, American multi millionaire Harold Vanderbilt introduced exciting new scoring bonuses in Bridge. With this change, 'Contract Bridge' was born.

Hilda and friend, 1963.

Hilda decided to sell her beautiful house which by this point was too big for her, and Raymond and she lived temporarily in a large flat on Albany Road. After school Raymond found himself uncertain of which direction he might like to take. The Grove family had always had a good nose and Hilda decided to recruit an old friend, Jack Pickthorn, who helped direct Raymond towards a career as a perfumer. After attending Lancing College in Worthing, Raymond went to work for International Flavour and Fragrance in London. Born of a merger in 1958, the company had been producing essential oils since the late 1800s where it obtained almond oil, cochineal and apricot kernels from Africa. At the time that Raymond went to work for them they had created synthetic ambergris and were finding ways to extract the odorous molecules from a living flower. Whilst he worked for them Raymond designed a fragrance called *Chantrelle* for Max Factor. When

Right: Hilda in New Zealand, 1970s.

Far right: Hilda on the *SA Vaal* at that prestigious moment of meeting the captain, 1970s.

Having fun with Marie and friends, 1970s.

he was 21 he moved out of the flat he shared with his mother and flew to New York before moving back to London in the early 1970s.

In 1972 Hilda moved alone to a new flat in Worthing. Having grown up in London she had always craved the sea and now she could sit and stare dreamily at it all day. There was a carpeted glass surround balcony with a comfy chair at both ends and a coffee table in the middle. A nest of three small pebble shaped tables sat in the corner. Hilda also passed the time by making tapestries, knitting and crochet, which she did whilst appreciating the sea views. She was also incredibly house proud and her flat was spotless without a speck of dust.

Over the next ten years Hilda devoted much of her life to travel, which she did extensively by air and sea. Every other year she visited her daughter Ann in New Zealand and Hilda flew until 1983 when she felt the plane journey was starting to upset her. She also frequently went on cruises, either alone or with her good friend Marie Edmondson from Bexhill. During the Seventies, they sailed to Durban on the *SA Vaal* and Hilda thoroughly enjoyed the experience, especially the spicy exotic food.

Hilda remained in constant contact with her son. During these years, Raymond was to have two significant relationships; the first with Sue, mother to Alexander, then with Eva, with whom he had Daniel and Simon. When Raymond was in his late thirties he was diagnosed with a brain tumour and initially after treatment he seemed to recover, only to suffer a relapse. Raymond died on 17th January 1990 aged 41.

The tragic loss of her beloved son was a double blow after having lost Jack only a few years before. Even though they had not been married for many years Hilda and Jack had always remained close and she always felt that he regretted leaving her and had never stopped loving her. At Raymond and Eva's wedding Hilda had been looking forward to spending some time with Jack and catching up with all their news but they were interrupted and never managed to talk alone. One of the things they were going to discuss was Jack going to stay with Hilda for a while but he never did as soon after this occasion Jack had a series of strokes and passed away. "He never really wanted to leave me and he still loved me when he died. I know he did. That lovely time that I had with Bill, well, it sort of spoilt my marriage because I couldn't go back to what I had. We just weren't compatible."

Hilda never had the sea or the seaside growing up poor in South London. Living in her flat

Far left: Raymond and Hilda, 1988.

Left: Hilda, Ann and her daughters Joanne and Jessica, 1990s.

in Worthing made Hilda very happy as she felt safe and content. She was 8 floors up in a secure block and it was a good place to be with good friends living in the same block. In 2005 Hilda had a fall and broke her hip. After spending some time in hospital she went home and had to get used to using a walker. Ann came to stay for five weeks so she could help build her up and cook for her but she knew it was time to move on when Hilda declared, "Now, look Ann! This is my kitchen!" Eventually though she found it hard to manage alone.

Ann now lives in Woolavington and is married to a taxi driver called Terry. She has a daughter who is still living and teaching in New Zealand and a son who teaches Natural Horsemanship at a ranch in Colorado. Terry and Ann were childhood sweethearts whose parents had known each other for years. They had not seen each other for 33 years until when visiting in 1989 Hilda told Ann that Terry's wife had died. This pulled at Ann's heartstrings and she instigated a meeting. With husband and son in tow, she saw Terry for the first time in years. Ann had been in an unhappy marriage for years so when Terry asked her if she was happy she replied "No! I'm coming home!" to which Terry said, "Come back to me!"

Hilda has been at Sydenham House for 3 years. The reason Ann found her mother a home in Bridgwater is because she had "come to appreciate that the people in Somerset are much warmer, kinder and friendlier, not at all like Londoners."

For Hilda it was difficult to leave her flat in Worthing but she is very happy and would not want to be anywhere else. When asked about how she feels about her life and reaching this grand age, she says "I'm living here now and all my thoughts are here. I don't think back any more."

Hilda's grandson Alex who is an opera singer and his girlfriend Louise, helping Hilda celebrate her 100th birthday.

ALICE HANSFORD

'Shut up, Alice I say to myself ... as long as I can do this, I will'

ALICE WAS BORN in 1909 in Street, Somerset to Mary and Walter Wells. She had three brothers, Walter, Sydney and Thomas – Thomas was the oldest and the most domineering and although not unkind he was the boss and his was the last word. She also had younger twin sisters who died when they were babies and one of Alice's earliest memories is seeing them in their coffins with coins on their eyes. Both of Alice's parents were lucky to have a job. Mary worked at Clarks Shoe Factory, stitching shoes whilst Walter worked at Tanners, processing the wet skins. The Wells children would play close to home in one of the adjoining fields. Alice went to a board school and particularly liked all the domestic subjects that basically taught her how to be a housewife. The children sat at individual desks with a small rounded inkwell in the corner. All the children were encouraged to take religious studies along with all the congregational duties, bible studies and singing in the Salvation Army choir. A couple of afternoons a week all the children gathered together to dance round the Maypole outside the chapel. During the first few years of school Alice has vague memories of the First World War and remembers that her grandfather was enlisted and that there were occasions that she cowered under a huge marble slab to shelter from the bombs.

After Alice left school at 14 she went to work in service for a while. In order to find a job she regularly went to the Labour Exchange and then visited the family seeking staff to obtain the full details. The first family she worked for were pleasant enough but she was naïve and unskilled, and was horrified when she was asked to draw and skin a rabbit. One of the first duties of the day was to boil the kettle so the lady's maid could take the lady a cup of tea. Then she had to clean the fireplaces and black the grates. She then swept and mopped all the floors and carried water to all the bedrooms for the wash stands. On some days she polished the brass and on others she cleaned the stone steps. Alice struggled for a while at this job but luckily didn't live with the family and would return home daily. She would be tired to the bone after working from seven in the morning without a break to only earn a meagre ten shillings, of which she gave her mother eight. Alice stayed with this family for six months but when they decided to move further up the country she refused to leave with them. The next family she worked for were much better. Mr and Mrs Tinian lived in Somerton and had a small daughter called Jane. They expected no more than cleaning and babysitting and Mr Tinian came and collected her and delivered her safely home. This was a happy time.

D.O.B. 20/07/1909

Family photo of Thomas,
Walter, Alice and Sydney
with their parents Mary and
Walter Wells, late 1940s.

Alice with Ken, Mary
and Ivor, 1995.

Alice and Lewis at
Christmas, 1993.

As a teenager Alice had many friends and was a mischievous playful girl, once betting her friends ten bob that she could roll down Wearyall Hill. She also enjoyed going to dances at Glastonbury Town Hall and her favourite dance was the Palaisglide. Normally walking home as late as midnight was never a problem but she remembers one episode when she had walked home with another friend who lived at the other end of Street. After saying goodnight Alice was just walking the last bit alone and she had to walk past a large swimming pool. In those days Alice had her sight and as she turned a corner she saw someone tall and big in the shadows and the figure started to move. She ran as fast as her legs would carry her and when she got to her front door, she banged her fist against the oak door screaming "Father, Father! There's somebody after me!"

The dances were usually the social hub of the week and generally seen as the best place to meet a young man. However this was not how Alice met her husband. Whilst shopping for oxtail and greens one day she found herself mildly interested by a young man in paint streaked overalls who happened to be examining the guttering on a three floored house on the corner of Compton Terrace. Never one to be shy, Alice started up a conversation. His name was Lewis and they were married in Shepton Mallet in 1928.

After a year of marriage, Alice and Lewis came off the Council waiting list and moved into their first home on the Mead. In 1929 Alice gave birth to baby Ivor and in 1933 a second boy, Ken, came along. The role of being a full time wife and mother would occupy most of Alice's time throughout the 1930s. The family lived in a small stone cottage that was cool in the summer and had a shaded garden with a pond full of frogs. Alice has fond memories of leaving the cottage and pushing the two boys in a large pram from her home in West Pennard to Haviot Corner with Smut the black cat following. One summer the whole family were haymaking in the fields. Her grandfather used to say he could cut an acre a day with the scythe and he'd cut the oats and barley with a hook. The children were all playing together as the grown ups pitched the hay up into the wagon with a fork. Ivor was six and was up on top of one of the shires playing with its mane. Suddenly the horse bucked and he fell off, breaking his arm. He had to have it strapped up with flat boards and had fun showing off his wooden arm for weeks. By the end of the decade, things were going to change as the outbreak of war was going to throw everything sky high.

Lewis was in the Royal Engineers and was sent to France. Lewis spent most of the war apart from Alice and although she would try to keep her family together, it was a struggle. Ivor went back to live with Grandma Mary on Compton Terrace until he was 16, helping to take some of the weight off Alice's shoulders. In 1941 when Lewis had a short leave at home, he and Ivor went to look at a new house and got caught in the middle of the blackout. It was pitch black when the sirens sounded and they sheltered in the darkened parlour. They moved to the house on Park Close and life in Street continued to be communal and cheerful even though there were bombs falling.

It seemed that a lot of evacuees from East London and Essex were sent to Street including a young Barbara Windsor. There were two or three Army camps in Street and many soldiers were stationed at Millfield School, which had been turned into barracks for the duration of the war. After the arrival of the evacuees there was a contingent of the Army to make way for further troops. First came the 'Glorious Gloucesters" and other regiments followed before being sent overseas. Many cultures would merge as Jamaicans, New Zealanders, Americans and Canadians lived amongst each other. For a while this gave a broader multi racial outlook to the people of Street, who had until then only been used to a certain culture. The cricket pitch on Farm Road was commandeered by the Ministry of Defence and about a dozen Nissen huts were erected to accommodate officers. The Americans came straight from Tilbury and they were stationed at Pursey's garage. They wore steel helmets with the strap hanging down and looked like they had stepped out of a John Wayne film. They gave dances for the local girls, parties for the children and there was also an endless supply of sweets and chocolates. The New Zealand troops were always a little unruly and were constantly reprimanded for climbing the monument in Glastonbury or throwing girls in the swimming pool.

Alice sunbathing in the garden of Tannery Close, 1960s.

Trip to Majorca, 1970s.

BARBARA WINDSOR

The Carry On films and its stars were a national institution. This long running series of low budget British Comedy films that mixed slapstick, farce and double entendres were loved by the nation between 1958 and 1978. Around twenty nine films were made by Pinewood Studios and the humour was in the British comic tradition of music halls and seaside postcards. It was all about the sending up of British traditions, customs and institutions such as the NHS in *Carry on Nurse/Doctor*, the monarchy in *Carry on Henry*, trade unions in *Carry On At Your Convenience* or beauty contests in *Carry On Girls*.

Barbara Windsor is best known for her roles in these films as well as playing East End matriarch and landlady Peggy Mitchell in *Eastenders*. Her East End roots are real as she was born in Shoreditch in 1937 and her father was one of the original costermongers, a real life barrow boy. She made her West End debut in 1952 in the musical *Love From Judy* and her first film role was in *The Belles of St Trinians* in 1954. In 1963 she received a BAFTA nomination for her role in *Sparrows Can't Sing*, a representation of life in the East End in the early Sixties. It was made on location in Limehouse and the set was often visited by Vallance Road residents, the Kray twins. She eventually came to prominence as the cheeky 'good time girl' in the Carry On films and her first role was in *Carry On Spying* in 1964. She starred in many over the next ten years and the scene she is most famous for is when she loses her bikini top during an aerobics session in *Carry On Camping*. After recently examining her family tree she has discovered that if she was to trace back 11 generations, she finds John Golding who is the great great grandfather of John Constable the landscape painter. This makes him Barbara Windsor's fourth cousin, six times removed.

Towards the end of the war Lewis returned to Alice and the family tried to pick up the pieces of their life in the aftermath of the horrors of the past six years. Lewis regained his former job working for the council and the boys were growing bigger every day. Ivor was now a young man who was earning a wage and soon to join the Army. It wasn't long before there was news of a new addition to the family but Alice had a lucky escape when one evening she took a tumble down some stone steps as they were leaving the cinema. They had gone to see *Gone with the Wind* and she wasn't looking where she was going, still in a swoon over Clark Gable. Alice thanked her lucky stars when in 1944 Mary was born and Alice's parents helped out to lessen the load.

Golden Wedding, 1978.

GONE WITH THE WIND

One of the greatest films ever made, it is one of the most enduring symbols of the Golden Age of Hollywood. This period in film history lasted from the end of the silent era in the late 1920s to the 1960s and films were prolifically issued by the Hollywood studios.

The book was first published in 1936 and was a romantic novel written by Margaret Mitchell, which won the Pulitzer Prize in 1937. The story is set in Clayton County, Georgia during the American Civil War (1861-1865). The title is taken from the poem *Non Sum Qualis Eram Bonae Sub Regno Cynarae* by Ernest Dowson: "*I have forgotten much, Cynara! Gone with the wind*". Scarlett O Hara also uses it when her home town is overrun by Yankees and she thinks of Tara, her plantation home, and whether that has also 'gone with the wind' that has swept through Georgia.

The film was produced by David O. Selznick who acquired the film rights for $50,000 which was a record amount for a first novel. Shot in three strip technicolour, the star studded historical epic was a classic tale of a love/hate romance. It starred Clark Gable and Vivien Leigh, a little known British actress whose billing was changed from 'presenting' to 'starring' when she won the Best Actress Oscar. Hattie McDaniel became the first African American to win an Academy Award for Best Supporting Actress for her portrayal of Mammie, Scarlet O Hara's maid. Max Steiner's sweeping musical score and the splendour and authenticity of the costumes and sets made it a spectacular production.

Hollywood was a hive of activity at the time of production. The director Victor Fleming was also working on the *Wizard of Oz* and the scriptwriter Ben Heche was working with the Marx Brothers on *At The Circus*. There was little time to eat in order to finish on time and people survived on bananas and salted peanuts. It met the deadline and when it opened just after the beginning of World War II it helped American audiences identify with the war story and its theme of survival.

In the late 1940s Alice found herself a job working as a cook in a school beyond Glastonbury. She had to walk two miles each way in all weathers wearing socks over her shoes when there was snow and ice on the road. She started work at seven in the morning and was one of a group of ladies who prepared and cooked the food. They made vast amounts of liver and bacon or shepherds pie, and for dessert the children had stewed prunes in white sauce or wobbly custard tarts. Every afternoon every work-table was scrubbed with boiling water. The children sat at long trestle tables with gingham table cloths and benches either side. A stack of chipped china plates sat at the end. At Christmas Alice made the puddings in tin baths, turning the mixture with a huge wooden spoon with a long handle. She often worked till past four in the afternoon and would then walk home and start again for the family, falling exhausted into her bed after midnight. This was a very hard and unhappy time for Alice and she looked forward to Tuesday mornings when she had the day off. On these days her brothers Tom and Walter would visit and they would drink tea and play cards. Another great pleasure that always cheered Alice up when she was feeling glum was singing with the Salvation Army choir, especially '*Oh you beautiful doll*' which was one of her favourite songs.

A trip to Jersey, 1995.

'OH YOU BEAUTIFUL DOLL!'

This ragtime love song was published in 1911 and was popular throughout the war years. The lyrics were written by Seymour Brown and the music was by Nat D. Ayer and Irving Berlin. The song featured in the 1928 musical *The Swing Party of 1928* and Judy Garland sang it in *For Me and My Girl* (1942). Ragtime enjoyed its peak between 1897 and 1918 and is characterised by its 'ragged rhythm'. It began as dance music in red light districts of American cities such as St. Louis and New Orleans. The *Maple Leaf Rag* was a hit for ragtime composer Scott Joplin and was influential for its melody lines and harmonies. Ragtime fell out of favour as jazz claimed the public's imagination after 1917, although there have since been numerous revivals.

Birthday party 100!!

During the 1960s Alice and Lewis moved to Tannery Close which was a warden-led home with detached bungalows and a block of flats. By now the children had left home and they had the opportunity to spend some time together. Sometimes on Thursdays they met friends at the British Legion where they would play bingo and have tea and ginger cake. For Alice it was a blessing that after all the years of slaving over hot stoves she could now relax and enjoy her life a little more. Soon after moving to Tannery Close Lewis took early retirement and they started going on outings organised by the over 60s club which was run by the local Community Centre. One of the trips was a coach trip to Gretna Green which she will never forget. A faux wedding had been staged and Alice and Lewis had been chosen to be the bride and groom. Costumes were laid on and Lewis looked handsome in a top hat and tails whilst Alice was a picture in the pale swirl of a summer dress.

Lewis passed away in 1992 but Alice continued to live in her flat for a further decade. Over the years Alice's eyesight has suffered terribly but taking a flight on Concorde is one of the happiest memories she has before she started to lose her sight. It was Friday May 26th 1995 and sheets of rain were hitting the tarmac hard. Alice, Mary and a lady called Vera waited in a large airy hangar and tea and biscuits were laid out on a makeshift table. The plane waited on the runway. This aviation icon that had first flown in 1969 stood majestically waiting for the passengers to board.

Five generations! Susan, Alice, great great grandson Thomas, Georgina and Ivor.

Mary had first noticed an advertisement in the *Bristol Evening Post* for flights from Bristol to Heathrow at subsonic rates. Knowing that her mother was in awe of this aeroplane she wasted no time in replying. Alice had always loved flying and when the family had taken holidays to Jersey she never minded the plane taking its time circling the sky whilst waiting to land as it meant she stayed in the sky longer. On this wet spring afternoon they were all led across the tarmac and climbed the steps. Alice was a little unsteady but determined. She sat in a window seat as the plane took off, gazing over a sky of clouds and absorbed in the delight of being in the belly of this incredible machine.

For Alice's 100th birthday the family hired a hall at the Victoria Club and 60 guests arrived, having travelled from all over the country. She was very excited to see Vera, her sister-in-law's daughter, as she hadn't seen her for some time. There was a sumptuous buffet laid on and an iced fruit cake. Each corner of the hall was filled with bunches of multi coloured balloons. Bottles of sherry lined the wall and the sound of champagne corks being popped rang out. The music was provided by old friends Trevor and Maureen who played old favourites on a Casio organ. These are the memories that keep Alice smiling as she sets herself comfortably in an armchair by an open window at Southlawns. Ever since losing her sight life has been quite difficult, but her family support and love her, and this is enough for now.

MABEL STUCKEY

*'At school I learnt about wild flowers,
and I have shared that knowledge my whole life'*

MABEL WAS BORN on 22 November 1907 in the parish of Long Sutton, in a house on Tengore Lane. Her mother was Ella Gooding and her father was Edwin Bennett. Mabel was the eldest of three with two sisters, Minnie and Irene and a brother, Fred. Her father was a stonemason in the quarries who dressed stones ready for them to be put down as pavements. When the First World War broke out he went to enlist, but was declined from service because he suffered from varicose veins. He continued to run a small holding where he reared cattle and grew potatoes.

Mabel's grandparents lived half a mile away and as there were no other houses nearby Mabel had no playmates other than her younger siblings. One of the chores they did was picking up stones from a grass field for a man who lived nearby. As a treat he would wait for the baker to come up the lane and then he brought in a bag of cakes for tea, throwing in two half-crown coins for good measure.

Mabel went to the Quaker school at Long Sutton and walked there alone, stopping on the way to pick up another girl. The classes at the Quaker school were small and relaxed and Mabel and her sister stayed at the Quaker school until she was nine. At this age her mother moved them to Langport Council School, as she felt they weren't learning what they should at the Quaker school. Ella didn't agree with the nature walks and the art classes but Mabel has passed on her knowledge of wild flowers and types of lichen because of them. There were slate and chalk for writing and boxes of sand to make gardens with flower heads, twigs and the other things the children had found on the nature walks. There was also a teacher who had a row of bottles and if unknown specimens were found the children would take them to her and she'd find the name of it. Mabel's favourite classes were history, drawing and sewing. There was a long strip of paper along the schoolroom wall with a cross section illustration of a ship and you could see all the rooms. The children were taught all about the mighty ocean liner and when *Titanic* sank everyone was very shocked.

Mabel was seven and learning the standards when the First World War started. All the pupils made their own cotton pinafores for school and if one of the dresses was threadbare at the front it would be saved to be worn at home. During playtime the children watched as army trucks came down the street with big canvas covers and soldiers would be sat along each side, waving and cheering. They could often be heard going along the top road from Taunton to Wincanton

D.O.B. 22/11/1907

Right: Brother Fred's Christening, 1916.

Far right: Grandma and Grandpa Goodings, 1930.

Mabel's mother outside the house on Tengore Lane that she was born in, circa 1920.

during the night. Mabel lived a hundred yards from the railway and when she heard the goods train coming they ran down to watch it pass. In the first carriage were the soldiers, in the second the horses and mules and the third was full of guns. There was an old workhouse nearby where German prisoners of war were held and sometimes the local farmers came and collected them in the morning and gave them work for the day, dropping them back in the evening.

After Mabel left school at 14 she stayed at home to help with the chores. When her sister Minnie left school she took over the housework and helped their mother, and Mabel was found work 'in service'. She worked for Mr William Kelway in a big house in Langport for six months looking after his daughter and helping the housekeeper with any other duties. At her next job she lived in with the family of a local doctor and looked after his children. Her mother made her uniform which was a black dress in the afternoon with a white apron. Mabel was treated like one of the family and had a little room near the laundry. When she had time she helped the parlour maid clean the silver or dried up the dishes, taking care with the fine china. Sometimes she helped the cook or did some darning. Mabel earned £1 a month of which 2 shillings had to go towards health insurance. She stayed there for 3 years and 3 months.

GIRLS FRIENDLY SOCIETY

Created in 1875 within the Anglican Church, the GFS is now an international organisation. Founded in England by Mary Elizabeth Townsend, its purpose was to provide a place for girls who were not married and who had been sent to the city by their families to work in textile mills. The Society would give girls the experience of friendship in a fellowship of Christian love and service. In 1877 the first branch of the GFS was established in America and in the late 1800s it helped support young women entering this country by providing housing and jobs. It also established the Travellers Aid Society and during the war, shelter and aid were found for refugees and funds were raised to help the Red Cross purchase ambulances. Today it is a national voluntary organisation in the Episcopal Church for young women aged between 5 and 21. The GFS motto is 'bear ye one another's burdens and so fulfil the laws of Christ' (Galatians 6:2).

Quaker school at Long Sutton, Mabel is second from right in the front row, 1915.

Mabel was a member of the Women's Institute and the Girls Friendly Society and the vicar's wife held the meetings in the church rooms in Langport. The girls played sewing games or did competitions and sometimes there would be a folk dance, although Mabel didn't go to many dances as she lived in quite a remote place. The bi-annual Sunday school outings to Weymouth or Brighton were always very popular and you made sure you had your name down early for these occasions. On one outing Mabel went to visit an aunt in Southampton and stayed for a couple of days, taking a boat over to the Isle of Wight for the day. Although she never went abroad she and her brother and sisters did once go up in a stunt plane. It was a bright Sunday afternoon and there was a show in a local field. A small biplane was performing stunts and the onlookers were given the opportunity to go up in the plane for the price of £1 for 5 minutes. They all jumped at the chance of doing something so exciting. Mabel knew she would have to go up with brother Fred as he was the darling of the family, and if anything happened to him there would be trouble and her life would not be worth living.

Mabel as a little girl.

BRIGHTON

One of the most vibrant, colourful and creative cities in Europe, Brighton is a town in East Sussex. The ancient hamlet of Brighthelmstone dates from before the Domesday Book when a rent of 4,000 herrings was established. It emerged as a health resort for sea bathing during the eighteenth century when Doctor Russell of Lewes prescribed seawater as a cure for a list of ailments. By 1780 the development of the Georgian terraces had begun and further growth was encouraged by the patronage of the Prince Regent who went on to construct the Royal Pavilion, noted for its oriental interior. It became a popular destination for day trippers after the railway arrived in 1841 and the Victorian era saw the building of many major attractions including the Grand Hotel and the Palace Pier. Brighton is sometimes referred to as 'London-by-the-Sea'.

Mabel met her husband Jimmy Stuckey at a social evening. He worked for a builder who repaired old houses and churches, including the towers of a church in Taunton. They were

Jimmy and Mabel's wedding,
June 6th 1938.

Mabel and Jim during
the war, 1940s.

married in June 1938. The following year the war started, but Jimmy carried on with his job until 1942 working on Huish School and different properties in Ilminster. The trees in his orchard were loaded with apples and he had just spent two months harvesting them when he was called up. Mabel's brother Fred was also called up for the 'Twenty Twos' where he would have operated wireless equipment on planes, but as he was colour blind he could not go.

Jimmy Stuckey was in the 15th Scottish Infantry and stayed in England until D-Day. He had spent a little time in a military hospital after having an accident in an Army vehicle and was then assigned to a variety of tasks for the war effort. He was stationed at Tilbury Docks, loading jeeps which were ready to land in France; he navigated barges, towing one behind the other, all the way to France, and he spent some time in Holland but was then sent home to learn how to sterilise water as they were testing the water in the canals.

Mabel stayed at home looking after the children. She had Grace in 1940 and when there were air raids Mabel protected Grace by putting her in a cane basket, placing another one on top like a lid. Jimmy always felt safest in bed. The year before Jimmy went to war in 1942, Mabel's first son Norman was born. Jimmy left on a Thursday morning and for the first few days little Norman cried "Daddy! Daddy!" every time the back door opened. Jimmy was in the Army for 2 years and 9 months.

Mabel was not short of company throughout this time. Her mother was staying with her as well as a sister and husband who stayed in another part of the house. Jimmy came home on leave occasionally, but Mabel often went for weeks without seeing him. The family got by and stretched the rations as best they could. They had a dozen hens and Mabel preserved the eggs in a big earthenware pot using a powder called 'isinglass' which became like crystals when it hardened. The eggs would be preferable in cakes and puddings rather than fried or poached. Generally people made cheap wholesome meals and Hitler had the audacity to advise that a 'one pot' meal was the thing to have. During the festive period there was room for improvisation: Plain cakes with a little icing; a fir branch stuck in a flower pot in place of a spruce tree; parched tongues from all the licking of paper chains; and the children gathered ivy and evergreens to drape over the mantelpiece and across the tops of paintings. At Quaker School Mabel was taught how to make Chinese lanterns and how to link them together with string and hang them around the room. A typical Christmas meal was a chicken and the raisins for the pudding were soaked in sherry and a sixpence and button thrown in the mix. Nobody wanted the button.

The war was terrifying. There were no sirens in the countryside but the planes still flew over. The first time Mabel saw them she looked out of the window and the sky was full of black spots. She thought there must be flies on the window but it was planes. There were bombers followed by fighters, and lots of puffs of smoke. It was about midday and they were going to bomb Filton. There is still a bullet hole in the shed roof from one of the fighters. Every evening at about six o'clock, the German planes would come over and they made a different noise like droning and were very high up. In the early hours of the morning Mabel would hear them going back, tired and spent in the night sky.

Jimmy Stuckey was one of the first British soldiers to take supplies into Belsen. Before the soldiers went in they were given a bottle of whisky each. The men weren't told anything about where to go or what they would encounter. As they approached the camp they noticed a strange

smell and a certain hush. There were no birds.
 As they got inside the gates of the camp they
saw a pile of dead bodies with children playing
around it. They had to go to the cookhouse and
a naked young woman came out and begged
them for water. They were not allowed to give
it as due to malnourishment and dehydration,
one sip of water may have killed them. They
now understood why they were given the
whisky.

Jimmy suffered with stomach problems for
the rest of his life and he never talked about
what he had seen. Grace discovered this
through a pile of paper cuttings and was
horrified. There was no counselling for
servicemen in those days and no such term as
Post Traumatic Stress Disorder.

After the war Jimmy was one of the first
soldiers to be demobbed, as builders were
needed to help rebuild the country. He worked
on the Merryfield airfield near Ilton which was

Mabel, Jim, Grace and Norman, 1940s.

a very heavy physical job. The men worked hard and were hungry after putting in long days.
Food shortages were even worse than during the war and Jimmy couldn't understand why he
couldn't have three rashers of bacon. One of the jobs that Mabel had to do was gardening and
tending of the land and when Jimmy received his demob money he bought a greenhouse, which
Mabel used to grow different kinds of produce.

With all the men returning home there were a lot of babies born just after the war and in 1946
Mabel had her third child, Brian. Grace was now five and had just started at Stembridge School
and Norman had just turned three. They received parcels from an aunt in America with cloth and
material that was like the hemp which the cattle feed was kept in. Mabel and Grace attempted to
make dresses with it from a pattern in a magazine. During this time Mabel's main purpose was
being a wife and mother, and also trying to be a father figure as Jimmy was busy at work and not
at home very often. Spare time was usually spent at home and the family never really went on
holiday. The most they did was spend a weekend with her brother Fred in Falmouth, usually
when there was a project for the men to do such as terracing the garden.

The family showed a great deal of creativity and versatility. Over the next ten years Mabel
was busy tending her garden and growing tomatoes and when they were ripe, a hand-written
sign would be placed outside the house offering 'tomatoes for sale'. At Christmas Jimmy grew
chrysanthemums and the children helped gather them into bunches, tying them with twine.
Mabel was to expand into growing bedding plants and took a lot of care over the tiny seedlings.
They also kept chickens and hens and when the egg man was coming, the kitchen table would
be piled high with dirty eggs to be cleaned and then packed into cardboard egg trays. By this time

Mabel, Jim and the boys at a cousin's wedding, 1951.

The whole family sometime in the Sixties. Grace, Mabel's daughter, is at the front holding the baby.

Mabel tending her garden, 1979.

Right: Sitting in the ruins of a stone hut in a prehistoric village on Dartmoor, Mabel, Kitty Bennett and her son Michael, 1980s.

Far right: Mabel's 100th Birthday with balloons and family after a lovely meal at the Rusty Axe in Stembridge.

Brian was at school but as soon as he got home he was out in the garden helping his mum and dad.

All the children were very bright and passed their 11 plus with no difficulties, going on to have varied careers. Grace went to teacher training college and taught Home Economics until changing to Special Needs; Norman joined Customs and Excise, then left the Civil Service and trained with airlines and then cargo. He worked around Heathrow Airport for many years as a Cargo Custom Liaison Officer, boasting that if someone needed to send an elephant to Timbuktu, he was your man; and Brian became a buyer of parts that are used in Ministry of Defence equipment.

During the 1960s Mabel continued with her thriving produce and plant business and also harvested the vast amounts of apples provided by the trees in her orchard. Jimmy and his youngest son worked tirelessly during the autumn months, gathering baskets of apples and carrying them to their old pick-up truck for the journey to the nearest cider press. Brian was now a strapping young man and very close to his father so it came as an enormous shock when Jimmy died suddenly of a cerebral haemorrhage at the age of 57.

For Mabel, her home was the centre of her universe and she never ventured far from it. In 1978 the orchard was razed and a bungalow was built for her. Stembridge had a small shop by the local pub, The Rusty Axe, and when the children were young the shopkeeper came on a Monday morning to take your order which was delivered later in the day. During the time of food shortages the ration book would be produced and a little tick or cross would go through that day's allowance. The butcher and baker came on Tuesdays and a little fish van on Fridays. If Mabel was feeling particularly adventurous she would take a bus into Yeovil on a Wednesday to look around the shops or pick up a few extras.

Family was always very important to Mabel and often she looked after her grandchildren Sarah and Becky when Brian's wife, Priscilla, was at work. They often presented Mabel with armfuls of dolls and demanded that she talk like them as she had a knack of imitating baby voices and cartoon characters. At Christmas her aunt and uncle came over from Long Sutton for lunch, then they left their daughters behind and cycled back to the farm to milk the cows, cycling back in time for tea. The evenings would be spent playing games and then they all had supper which consisted of cold meats, pickles, stilton and a bottle of port. On Boxing Day they would go to

Long Sutton and do it all again.

Mabel has had a love of painting since she was old enough to hold a pencil. Whilst at school she drew avidly and now she proudly displays her paintings on the walls of her sitting room. She loves knitting and made the rug by the fire and the embroidered fire screen before she was married. Mabel also adores cats and would love to have another one but realises it might be impractical as she finds it so hard to bend over.

Mabel can still read the paper without her glasses although she does have a cataract. She is a natural communicator and has kept diaries all her life, noting things like 'the coalman came today' or that a bank statement had arrived. She writes regularly to her brother who lives in Dawlish and her sister who lives in a care home in Swindon. She has also kept all the letters that Jimmy wrote to her.

Although still fiercely independent, Mabel became ill in 2009 and was taken into hospital for a short while. She has recovered well but is fairly arthritic and cannot really cope with cooking meals and certain household duties. Her son Brian lives in the original house next door and takes on the carer duties one weekend a month but Grace is her main carer and lives with her most of the time, going home to Poole every 5th weekend. Since June, Theresa and other carers have come and given Mabel her meals and anything else she needs.

Mabel with her first great-granddaughter Abigail in 1997.

Reminiscing past times (and childhood days) with some old photographs – Mabel is 101 and brother Fred is 94, 2009.

LADY MARGARET TREDGOLD

'The best stories can never be told!'

MARGARET WAS BORN in Kimberley, South Africa on August 30th 1910, the eldest of seven sisters. Her parents were Colin Cuthbert Baines and Helen Buden, who originally wanted to become a missionary but instead became a kindergarten teacher. Margaret's grandfather had moved to South Africa during the Boer War which was fought between Britain and the two independent Boer republics, the Orange Free State and the South African Republic. After the war he decided to stay in South Africa and make a fresh start. He joined the Cape Mounted Police in the wake of the diamond rush which followed the first discoveries.

Kimberley is the capital of the Northern Cape and was originally called New Rush after the first clamber for diamonds. Margaret's childhood was spent in the small towns of Lady Grey and Aliwal North amidst beautiful countryside by the Orange River. This is the longest river in South Africa and rises from the Drakensburg Mountains and it was on these very banks that the first 'Eureka' diamond was found in 1867. This was an idyllic place to grow up and the girls had plenty of freedom as long as they stayed in pairs. It was a hard walk to school especially during the bitter snowy winters, so their mother sent them off with hot potatoes in their pockets to warm their cold hands. The girls started their education together in a small village school and then Margaret went to a boarding school in Weinberg, Cape Town, which was several days journey away. She really disliked this school and hated living to the sound of bells. She found boarding school very restrictive and was in an all-white class as the African children went to school in their own townships. Margaret was the only one of the sisters to go to this school and she thoroughly enjoyed English although art was to become a lifelong passion, which she took as a subject in place of Latin. When she was 13 she started at Cape Town Art School and felt very independent as she would walk there alone. Her art teacher often took the children out into the streets of Cape Town or to the surrounding countryside for them to paint and sketch whatever captured their attention.

After leaving school at 16 Margaret went and joined a teacher-training course in Grahamstown. This was an Eastern Cape Province and the site of Rhodes University which was one of the four oldest universities in the country. She was there for two years and become a qualified primary school teacher specialising in art. Her first placement after qualifying was in a pretty seaside town called East London which lies on the Indian Ocean coast between the Buffalo

D.O.B. 30/08/1910

Capt. Colin Baines and
Helen Baines, 1930.

Margaret aged ten
(2nd from left) with
her mother and sisters.

River and the Nahoon River. She shared a flat with a friend and the girls were very independent spending time on the sand dunes and swimming in the turquoise sea that lapped the edges of the 'Sunshine Coast' in their spare time. Before long however she was packing her bags, as she had been offered a job in Rhodesia. This is where she would meet her first husband Bill Phear.

THE FOUNDING OF RHODESIA

Modern Rhodesian history dates back to the Matabele journey from the Transvaal in the late 1830s when they arrived in the area known as Bulawayo. The Matabele, a descendant of the Zulu nation, were a predatory race. Their intrusion of the land north of the Limpopo marks the first retaliation with white settlers in Southern Africa and the impact it would have on the course of Rhodesian history.

The first white people to reach Rhodesia were hunters, trekkers and missionaries who crossed the Limpopo in search of good grazing land and David Livingstone was the first explorer to reach Victoria Falls in 1855. The Scramble for Africa started by the discovery of gold and diamonds was going to be a catalyst for rebellion. The dominant African power on the Zimbabwe plateau in the 1880s was the Matabele Kingdom ruled by King Lobengula and white prospectors needed his permission to search for gold. One such man was Cecil John Rhodes.

The origins of land grabs started in a way with Rhodes. After failing to make his fortune in diamond mines he built the De Beers Consolidated Mining Co and continued to use the company's funds to acquire African land. The next step was starting the British South Africa Company and backed by Rothschilds he asked the British Government for a Royal Charter, giving him permission to colonize Central Africa under the consent of the British Flag. This in effect gave Rhodes total control in a volatile region.

In October 1888 King Lobengula signed what he thought was a limited mineral concession bill which gave certain parties the right to dig for gold and other minerals on his territory. When access to additional parts of his territory was requested King Lobengula became suspicious that the British wanted to colonise his land, and refused access to certain areas. Subsequently an invasion took place that culminated in the burning of Bulawayo. Although Cecil John Rhodes never settled in the colony it was named Rhodesia in his honour.

It wasn't until she was in her early twenties that Margaret would get to know Bill, although there had always been a link between their two families. They returned to the family home of Lady Grey to marry in the summer of 1935. It was a family tradition to hold the wedding at six in the morning and an old friend from Rhodesia led the vows. The ceremony took place in the Anglican village church and was followed by a sumptuous wedding breakfast.

Bill already owned a house but it was quite a distance from town so as their were no local jobs Margaret had to give up work. She started up an early Women's Institute group and a book club and in 1938 had her first child, Shirley. This was followed by her son Patrick in 1940 and another son, Stephen, in 1942. Bill was a very successful lawyer and a partner in a law firm but once war broke out all the men left along with a large movement of the Rhodesian African Army, as it was a British Colony. Bill was an officer and stationed on the Gold Coast for the duration of the war.

Far left: Wedding day for Margaret and Bill, 1935.

Left: Margaret and friend Durban Davies, 1941.

At some point he contracted chronic malaria and although he wasn't bedridden he was treated in a local hospital. For more than one reason this was a really worrying time for both of them.

During this time Margaret was never idle and contributed to the community in a number of ways. She started up one of the first nursery schools in a stone hut, which led the way for others to follow her example. They also bought goods and packed food packages to be sent to relatives in Britain. Margaret also founded the first library with a group of friends by collecting books from far and wide. There were piles of dog-eared paperbacks and pristine hardbacks on many subjects such as general interest, history, and literary classics. This was a worthwhile and productive input by all the women while the men were away, and was only possible because of the close network of friends who linked up together for the good of the community.

After the war most of the clients in Bill's law firm had found other lawyers to represent them, and as he didn't want to work in an office any longer they decided to start a farm. They moved to Marandella as it was the centre of Rhodesia's large forestry and farming district and chiefly marketed timber, beef, dairy and tobacco (one of the main industries in Rhodesia). Bill's brother Horace had his own long-established farms and as he was a director of one of the many tobacco auction houses he was able to give them plenty of advice. Tobacco was still a very popular crop

Bill and Shirley, 1939.

Right: Margaret and Shirley on the tobacco floors in Salisbury, 1959.

Far right: The boys, Patrick and Stephen at Carlyon Farm, 1951.

as this was well before the days of the smoking ban and although many farmers grew other crops, tobacco was the only type of farming that yielded extremely high profits. Tobacco farming was highly skilled work and it was a fantastic feeling if you took your crop into the sales and got a top price at auction. Margaret remembers how she rushed to see the price she had got for her crop, straining to hear over the 'sing song' voices of the auctioneers and how a good quality leaf looked slightly golden green and felt silky like a kid glove.

Margaret and Bill bought some land in Marandella to grow tobacco and went pioneer farming into what was still wild country. It was a big area of open land and woodland that smelt of eucalyptus and initially they had to live in a hut, which was normal practice when starting a farm. Bill built a temporary cottage and later he and Margaret built a family home on the farm which they called Carlyon. They cut their own roads and cleared the fields, cutting the trees down to prepare the ground. They grew seed beds down by the river and that was where young seed beds were prepared for planting. When the crop was ready it was baled on the farm and then the bales went to auction. They had a small crop but it was very high quality.

The community was very close knit. They lived near an African reserve and had between 40 and 50 workers who helped to get the initial business underway. The children went to a little village school called Digglefold, travelling about 10 miles to it every day by car. They loved this journey and spent it singing bush songs and spotting hoopoe birds or wild flowers that were tucked into rocks. The school was individual and quite unique and was run by a man called Colonel Pearce. He'd had a fairly miserable time at school and was determined that children would have fun. He did everything to make lessons interesting including lots of singing, and you could even bring your pet into class.

Margaret and Bill ran the farm for fourteen years, eventually selling it as Bill wanted to return to practising law. He started up the first legal law firm in Marandera, which was a small town for the farming community and one of the earliest centres of white settlement. By now it was the early 1960s and they built a house on the outskirts of town and led an established life, becoming leading figures in the community. Margaret started up another branch of the Women's Institute and the first nursery school in town. She also illustrated several books including the *Wild Flowers of Rhodesia* which was presented to the Queen Mother in 1953, and Margaret had the opportunity to meet her at Balmoral and in Zimbabwe.

During his time on the farm Bill had contracted Polio and although he had tried farming from the back of a wagon it was to prove far too difficult. He had been admitted to an isolation hospital during the height of the Polio outbreaks in the 1950s when hospital wards were filled with rows of iron lungs, which were machines that helped patients breathe when normal muscle control was lost. Bill died in 1970. After his death Margaret moved into the centre of Marandella to a house on Jelliman Avenue, which she designed and had built for her.

In the early 1970s Margaret married for the second time. Margaret Phear and Robbie Tredgold had been friends for years, and although she had known his first wife Lorna very well they had moved in very different social circles. Sir Robert Tredgold was one of the first generation of white Rhodesians, an original Rhodes scholar and Chief Justice of the Federation of Rhodesia and Nyasaland. The Tredgolds were an eminent respected couple who held an elevated position within the community. They were part of a busy social whirl whereas the Phears had lived a more rural lifestyle on the farm. As their lives changed and both of them lost their partners, they became close. When Robbie asked Margaret to marry him she asked the children if they minded, as if they did they would just remain friends.

By this time the children had their own lives. Patrick was in America as he and his wife Virginia had decided to have a fresh start and he was doing research and family mediation. Stephen went into business and still lives in Zimbabwe. Shirley went into teaching and had her first child in 1966. There was never going to be any animosity from them as they adored Robbie, which made him very happy as he and Lorna had never had any children. Margaret and Robbie were married in the local Catholic church by a very old friend of Margaret's and it was a very happy occasion. Family and friends attended and the reception was held in the garden with a buffet luncheon. The event was kept fairly quiet as Robbie didn't want the press to find out. They had decided to settle in the Jelliman Avenue house and for a short while they had tremendous fun. They travelled to America and England, visiting relatives and just enjoying their life together. Sadly the dream was not to last long as Robbie died in 1977 following an asthma attack. They had been married for just four years.

After the pain of losing Robbie, Margaret went back to teaching art. She found a position at the prestigious Nagal House but also did

Sir Robert Tredgold.

Wedding day for Robbie
and Margaret, 1975.

Stephen, Shirley, Margaret
and Patrick, 1991.

volunteer teaching in African townships. Her pupils were junior school children and this was virgin ground as some of them had never held a paintbrush before. They achieved wonderful results and regularly held exhibitions, selling fairly primitive paintings in order to buy paper and paints. Within Rhodesia the communities ran parallel to each other and each respected the other, unlike the situation in South Africa. The whites were more dominant and could be quite bombastic but they helped the country to develop. Shirley remembers these as happy times when all races lived in harmony. By now Shirley was running a multi racial nursery school which included the children of the African scientists from the research centre nearby.

The years of sanctions just before Robert Mugabe came into power were very hard. As far as the world could see the white Rhodesians were colonial whites who weren't letting black people get along fast enough. When Ian Smith, leader of the Rhodesian Front had declared the country independent from British rule in 1965 he stirred up a hornet's nest. The International Community had condemned this action and sanctions were imposed. In a way it made the country stronger as the people of Rhodesia were determined not to rely on other countries, instead getting along by themselves although most forms of trade or foreign exchange were forbidden. It made the country what it was and helped it to become 'the bread basket of Africa'.

In 1980 independence was granted and Rhodesia became Zimbabwe. The country had found itself a new president in Robert Mugabe who at first was a brilliant politician. It was only a matter of time before money started pouring into the country from all over the world. The schools and the health system started to improve but not the farming. Then the Mugabe reign started to turn sour and he began to take all the country's wealth for himself.

MUGABE AND THE BREAD BASKET OF AFRICA

Robert Gabriel Mugabe was born in the Zvimba District in Southern Rhodesia and was the son of a carpenter. Raised with Catholic ideals, he was an introspective boy who spent long hours alone reading books. He qualified as a teacher and earned six further degrees, two whilst in prison. His political career began when he joined the National Democratic Party in 1960 and first clashed with Ian Smith. By 1963 he had joined a rival party, the Zimbabwe African National Union (ZANU) who were guided by Africanist and Maoist ideals. In 1964 he was arrested for subversive speech and spent 11 years in Salisbury Prison. This made him and his followers stronger, and whilst in prison he became leader of ZANU. Mugabe's political viewpoint was that, "a new progressive society could not be constructed on the foundations of the past and that they would have to destroy most of what had been built up after 1900 before a new society based on subsistence and peasant values could be constructed". In April 1979 the first democratic election in rechristened Zimbabwe's history took place and 64% of black citizens lined the streets to vote. People believed that this was a new beginning.

Mugabe led the liberation movement against white minority rule and was elected into power as head of Government in 1980. He has since carried the title of President and Executive Head of State and has been constantly re-elected by his people. This may slightly counteract the numerous claims of widespread vote rigging, election fraud and intimidation. Land Reform has been a desperate issue in Zimbabwe's recent bloodied history. When Zimbabwe gained independence, 46.5% of the country's arable land was in the possession of 6,000 trade farmers while white farmers owned 70% of the best farming land. As part of an agreement any land distribution was blocked for ten years. From the beginning of 2000, an extra condition in a new referendum was designed to allow the Government to seize white owned land for redistribution to black farmers without compensation. Even though the vote failed, war veterans started invading white-owned farms and people were living in fear of their lives. Since these actions agricultural production has crashed and the economy is ruined. Once the 'bread basket' of Southern Africa, Zimbabwe now depends on international food aid and support from outside to help feed its people and save the country from disaster.

During the 1980s Lady Margaret stopped teaching and started to write and illustrate children's books on a more full time basis. During the Second World War the Royal Air Force had been at a training camp in the local town to practise what would happen if they were shot down by enemy fire and were often taken to remote parts of the country. Margaret made friends with one of these men, Robert Martineau, an Anglican priest and botanist who years later became a bishop. He was fascinated by the wild flowers that he was finding in this new country and when he was out on training he would pick them and bring them back in a half dead state and ask Margaret to draw or paint them. He was writing about them and pressing them to take back to Cambridge.

The first book of *Rhodesian Wild Flowers* which included her illustration was published under her maiden name. She will sit and look at one of her books with her daughter and exclaim, "Here! Look at this darling plant. I can still remember where we found it" as she remembered the orchid tucked into a crevice in the rocks that she noticed while taking the children to school. She also wrote stories for children that were re-workings of African legends and folk tales and she continued to do this until 2008. Margaret's two great loves will always be children and art.

At the beginning of 2000 Margaret came to England. She had been living in sheltered housing run by the Boredale Trust but the situation in Zimbabwe was becoming too difficult. Shirley and her husband had intended seeing the chaos through, not wanting to be chased out of their home by marauding gangs, but after being very badly burgled, local towns set on fire and both of them being beaten, they decided they had just enough funds in England so they left. Both of their sons were already in England and soon after they arrived her mother e-mailed to say she was coming. Shirley was delighted and Margaret went to live with them at their house in Puckington, a small village in Somerset. In 2004 Margaret moved to Muchelney House, a sheltered housing complex in Ilminster where she has a delightful flat that looks onto the green rolling hills of Somerset and her family nearby.

IVY ADLER

'All I wanted to do was have babies!'

IVY WAS BORN on December 2nd 1911 in Lymington, New Forest. Her father was from Ipswich and when he was a young man he travelled all over the country to look for work. Ivy's father was put into contact with the brother of Lord Allenby, who wanted someone to look after the horses which he used at his laundry, and when Ivy was a girl her father told her a ghost story about his time working there. One cold bright morning he was sent to tend to the horses and it was early, as the ladies were on duty doing the ironing. Ivy's father used to light the stove and on this particular morning he heard footsteps and called out but there was no answer. Suddenly two big wicker baskets of laundry tumbled from a height onto the floor, which was strange as normally it took two men to lift one. That day all the machinery failed and the belts wouldn't work.

The day to day running of the laundry was hard work as well as looking after the horses but he was certain to meet Ivy's mother, who was visiting her mother (who was a colleague) and they were bound to be introduced. After they were married Ivy's mother was employed to iron all the officers' wives' blouses; she was a beautiful ironer and would never let Ivy do the ironing, even after she'd had her first baby.

Ivy was three when the First World War broke out and she remembers one occasion when her mother pointed at a plane high in the sky, and another time when they saw the gigantic hulk of a Zeppelin, shrouded in cloud. Her father did try to enlist but he was a small man and when he was driving the army trucks he couldn't see over the top of the car bonnet, so he was kept at the laundry dealing with the officers' clothes while his wife did the ironing. When Ivy was older her father found a job working for the Electric Light Company, and their house in Lymington was one of the first to have electric light. He died in an accident at work one day when he bent forward and unknowingly touched his head against a live wire.

Ivy went to a little school on the other side of the water. It was a long walk through a little village and past the pier, from where the Isle of Wight ferry sailed. Ivy was a small delicate child and the doctor thought it was too much of a walk for her so he persuaded her parents to enrol her into a different school. She had to walk down to the water's edge and take a little boat that took her down to a quay; then she had to climb two hills and ended up walking further than she had to her other school. However she loved school and her favourite subjects were English and poetry. On one occasion she won a copy of the *Swiss Family Robinson* when she wrote a poem about her mixed up

D.O.B. 02/12/1911

Above left: Ivy and Thomas on their wedding day in 1931.

Above right: Ivy aged 17.

Ivy with baby Gladys and Jean as a toddler, 1933.

terrier Jack, … *'my dog Jack he's not much to look at and neither am I. If one lost the other, the other would die.'* She and Jack were the same age when he died.

Although she was quite a solitary child, she made good friends with Olive Ayles and Mollie St. John and they would sit on the stone steps outside the chapel while Ivy taught them cat's cradle with garden twine. Ivy was an only child and when her parents went to Southampton sometimes to watch the football or do some shopping, she would stay with her grandmother. Here she would spend hours on her grandmother's crystal set which was a simple radio receiver that needed no batteries but instead ran on the power given out by radio waves. She enjoyed listening to London 2LO, which had been broadcasting since May 11 1922 for just one hour a day, and was only the second radio station to regularly broadcast in Britain. She loved all the tunes and knew all the words and one of her favourites was 'The Clown's Baby' which she bought from Woolworths in Southampton.

When Ivy left school she went to help a friend and her disabled mother before getting a job in a preparatory school at Milford on Sea. Ivy's life revolved around the Congregational church in Lymington, where she joined the Girl Guides and then later became a Sunday school teacher and sang in the church choir. She would look forward to the annual trips to places like Bournemouth where you spent what coins you had on a cup of tea and maybe a sticky bun.

One day she was delivering some sheets for her mother and was taking a short cut along the platform of the local station as a train pulled in, and a young man stepped down from a carriage. He caught her eye and winked, and that was it. Thomas was a plasterer and had come from Merthyr Tydfill looking for work, having been unemployed for two years. Britain was still recovering from World War I and as a result there was a great deal of financial instability, heightened by the Wall Street Crash in 1929 which shook the world. By the end of 1930 unemployment had doubled, which led to a Conservative landslide in the general election the following year. In this landscape of uncertainty, Thomas had come to Lymington as there was a job on a building site. He was a great footballer and played for a Welsh team, and Ivy was smitten by his good looks and trim physique. Ivy's parents were very strict generally but they approved of Thomas and gave her their blessing. Ivy and Thomas would go to the cinema or for long walks with a picnic basket full of scones and hard boiled eggs. After four months they were engaged and two years later they were married.

Ivy and Thomas lived in a little cottage down by the river in Lymington, renting until they were able to get a council house. As far as Thomas was concerned there was no need for Ivy to work, which was fine for her as all she wanted to do was have babies.

Over the next 20 years Ivy had nine children - Jean was the first baby and was born three weeks overdue in 1931 at the height of the Depression. Between then and the war breaking out she had four more babies - Gladys in 1933, Baden in 1936, Valerie in 1937 and Josephine in 1939.

During the war Thomas was in the Royal Army Medical Corps and went all over the country until he was eventually stationed in India. This specialist division of the British Army provided medical services to all British Army personnel. Thomas was sent to train at Cookham Camp for six months and was only permitted to use his weapon in self-defence. Ivy always thought he looked terribly smart in his navy blue beret and silver belt buckle.

Late one evening tragedy hit Ivy's family when Baden died of gas poisoning at the age of ten. He was going to have a bath and used a little gaslight to heat the water, which appeared to have malfunctioned whilst he lay soaking in the warm water and he suffocated. At the time Ivy had no idea that someone could die in this manner and it makes her bitter even now. She feels that today people would know what to do in such circumstances, such as laying a child down and keeping them warm, but at the time she knew nothing. All she could do was drag him out of the bath and run for help to the policeman who lived just over the road. Thomas was away in India when Ivy lost Baden and she had to write and tell him that his son had died.

After the war things were tough as there was very little money around. Thomas was now home from the war and Ivy had eight hungry mouths to feed following the births of Johnny in 1941, Diane in 1944, Glynes in 1947 and Meryl in 1950. Despite her quiet family upbringing there had always been a lot of children around. Her grandmother had ten children of her own and then took on five children who had been orphaned. Grandma and Grandpa Winkworth were originally from London and were adored by all the children. She was a midwife and he was a fisherman and when Ivy was a girl she went fishing for bass and eels with her father and grandpa. This love of fishing was passed on to her children and they would stop at the butchers for a marrowbone and then go down to the banks of the river, put the bone on the end of a piece of string and dangle it in the water, hoping that a crab would take the bait. They also went winkling and Ivy would boil them up in a big pot. Once, Thomas caught a big skate and the children were too scared to go into the bathroom as he'd left it flapping around in the bath.

By the early 1950s Ivy had had the last of her babies and the eldest children took on more responsible roles, helping her with the younger ones. It seemed a myth that a large family was more work, as the children helped to bring each other up and when Jean got married she took on the role of second mum to her brothers and sisters whenever she came home. When Ivy was 44 she had an ectopic pregnancy and had to have a hysterectomy. This was the end of her child-bearing days but she would still have her hands full for many years to come.

Thomas continued to work as a plasterer and when the children were old enough they went out to work, as there were many mouths to feed and any contribution to the housekeeping jar was appreciated. The family didn't have a car and walked everywhere or took the bus. They still enjoyed going to the cinema and Ivy was a great fan of Spencer Tracy. There were three changes of film a week, one on a Sunday and two during the week. Valerie remembers when there was an A-film showing she would stand on the steps and ask a complete stranger to take her in, which would be an unthinkable act today.

SPENCER TRACY

Starring in more than 70 films between 1930 and 1967, nominated for nine Oscars and winning two, this versatile and natural actor was one of the greatest film actors of our time. Born in Milwaukee in 1900, he was a wild restless boy who was expelled from many schools before he

The whole family.

Ivy and Diane, 1945.

Jean and baby Gladys, 1934.

Ivy, Tom and Valerie on Hillside Road, Lymington, 1958.

Ivy and her girls, 1968.

discovered his true calling. After appearing in a play called *The Truth* at Ripon College, he decided on a career in acting. He studied acting in New York and went on to star in six Broadway plays before Hollywood beckoned. In 1935 he signed with MGM, the most dominant studio in Hollywood, and he won an Academy Award for Best Actor two years in a row for his roles in *Captains Courageous* in 1937 and *Boys' Town* in 1938. He shares this record with Laurence Olivier.

Spencer Tracy and Katherine Hepburn were a close screen pairing but their personal life was often scrutinised, although they always chose to not speak publicly about their private life. They had a complex relationship that started in the early 1940s during the filming of *Woman of the Year* and continued throughout nine films until his death in 1967. The last film they appeared in was *Guess Who's Coming to Dinner*, which was a groundbreaking film as it tackled the issues surrounding inter racial marriage. Filming ended just seventeen days before his death and Katherine Hepburn was never able to watch the film as the memories were too painful.

In 1952 London hosted the Queen's Coronation and Ivy went to watch the parade with Thomas. They stayed overnight with an aunt in Twickenham and met Johnny in town, as he had been on a school trip and was being dropped off at an appropriate place to meet his parents. They all went on one of the open-air buses so they had a great view, and Ivy remembers seeing the Queen of Tonga go by in a glittering coach and horses, draped in all her finery, on the way to Westminster Abbey. Ivy was so excited that she was hanging over the side of the bus. When they bought their first television a couple of years later, a black and white Pye set for £84, everyone on their street wanted to come around and watch it whenever there was a special ceremony or occasion.

By 1960 Valerie had married and moved to Southampton and Ivy had her first two grandchildren, Ian and Ross, who helped replace Ivy's babies who were now grown up. Ivy cycled everywhere and took her shopping home this way, hanging a shopping bag over each handle bar and balancing one on the back if she could. She knew that her grandmother had shopped for ten on a bike so she wasn't doing anything incredible.

It was now the 1960s and Glynes and Meryl were engrossed in the 6:5 Special on television. Ivy would find herself humming the theme tune as she peeled potatoes on a Friday for fish pie, 'Time to jive on the old 6:5'. This was the BBC's attempt at the first popular music show, using a thin blonde disc jockey called Pete Murray. The audience of young people filled the studio space and thin girls in mini skirts with eyes circled with kohl danced to the likes of Petula Clark, Marty Wilde and an odd bunch called the Eden Street Skiffle Group.

Ivy realised that times were changing and that young people had more freedom and energy, and it was only a matter of time before the last of her babies would leave home. Meryl had always been a little unorthodox but Ivy was unprepared for the lifestyle she would adopt. All of Ivy's other children had followed the conventional route of courting, marriage and then leaving home to start a family but Meryl was not going to conform to this set piece. At the age of 18 she left home to go and live with some friends in London where she found a job in a bank and the girls found a flat to share. Ivy was horrified.

In the early 1970s retirement loomed for Thomas, and one of the first things he and Ivy did was to book a mini cruise to Bilbao after Ivy had seen an advert in the magazine *TitBits*. This was one of the first times that Ivy had danced. Always an agile man, Thomas was also a wonderful dancer but he had never taken her dancing before. The tiny dance floor onboard helped her fulfil a dream and she was happy to be swept around the floor by her husband. Thomas had always been quite possessive of Ivy and if anyone dared use her first name he would exclaim, "It's Mrs Adler to you!" Not only had Ivy never had the option of a career but if she had wanted to spend time with a friend, Thomas would get jealous and dominant. Lucille was another good friend and they had gone shopping together with their bags on the bike handles. Her husband worked nights and slept during the day and once a week Ivy would spend the whole day with Lucille, but she always had to be home by the time Thomas returned from work. He didn't like to think that she was having a life of her own or enjoying herself when he was at work, not even visiting her daughters who wouldn't tell him that Ivy had been to see them. Ivy had to make sure that she caught the bus by two pm as Thomas could be quite nasty if he was disobeyed.

After suffering a few small strokes Thomas was quite frail so he and Ivy moved to Ashley to be nearer to Jean. They were there for five years and Thomas passed away in 1981. Just two months before, Valerie had lost her husband and this brought mother and daughter even closer. After the initial shock of losing her husband, Ivy felt more free than she had in years and embarked upon a phase of travel that started with a trip to Canada.

Ivy had met her friend Maggie in the 1950s when she had come over from America with her family, as her husband had a job with the Esso Company. The day she first met Maggie had started uneventfully, until she saw a small child running down the road. Ivy asked the child her name and who she was but the little girl was too young to explain. She eventually found out that the family had only just moved to the area and the little girl had been playing with her brother and sister but had run away. The little girl's mother was Maggie and they became good friends, although within a few years Maggie moved back to America. Years later, just after Thomas had died, Ivy took a plane to Edmonton in Canada to visit friends and then on to Newark in New Jersey to visit Maggie. They also took a trip to Manhattan and spent a lovely time together visiting all the tourist attractions in New York. Ivy particularly adored the skating rink at the Rockerfeller Centre and the enormous Christmas tree adorned with shimmering baubles the size of footballs. Ivy thinks back poignantly to her visit to the Twin Towers and when she stepped out of the elevator at the top of the Empire State Building, she thought to herself, "if my girls could see me now".

When Ivy was 88 she went to live with Valerie, as she needed to use a wheelchair and Valerie's home was better suited. All her girls were there for her now with Diane drawing money out of her post office account for her and buying her whatever she needed. Her daughters have been there ever since and in the last ten years Ivy and Valerie have done a lot of travelling, visiting Austria, the West Country, and Jamaica Inn on Bodmin Moor. In May 2010 Valerie had to have a hip replacement operation and Ivy realised that she was now going to be too much of a burden. Valerie also realised that she and her mother were getting older so when Ivy herself suggested moving into Sunningdale Lodge, she agreed. The days are never quiet now as Ivy always has a stream of visitors and she occupies a very special place in all of their hearts.

Croyde Bay, 1973.

Ivy with her grandson
Alistair, 2009.

VINCENT COOPER

'Would you believe it?'

D.O.B. 22/11/1911

VINCENT WAS BORN on November 22nd 1911 in the village of Wombwell near Barnsley, South Yorkshire. It was here that the first recorded case of scrying (crystal gazing) was confessed to in 1467 and this small village in the heart of the Dearne Valley also has a history of coal mining. The 'black gold' from the Yorkshire coalfields was the major source of power behind the Industrial Revolution of the eighteenth & nineteenth centuries. Vincent's father Walter worked in the coalmines and Vincent remembers his great uncle Owen leading the pit pony through the village. The golf course in Wombwell used to be known as the 'hillies' and was once a thriving pit, until in 1857 a large explosion brought death and misery to the area called Landhill and 189 men were killed.

Vincent was the eldest of five children and he lived at 49 Roebuck Street, a small house on a tired and run-down estate. Times were hard and people lived hand to mouth but this made the community stronger. Life seemed to revolve around the pits and when the children were young they would jump into the canal and come out blacker than when they went in. They then took the short cut home, dripping wet as they ran past Woods Glassworks and along the side of the canal just west of Station Lane. After they'd scrubbed the soot off their bodies the boys would cycle to the speedway track, with Bobby the West Highland terrier chasing after them.

When Vincent left school he was determined not to work in the coal mines so he did a variety of jobs, even though as the 1930s approached he was very lucky to find work as many people were unemployed. He had various painting and decorating jobs and his father knew the owner of the local public baths, a lively chap called Jack Mitchell who offered to find Vincent work. During the summer he had a job as a pool attendant and on Friday and Saturday nights during the winter months he acted as a door attendant at local dances. This was the perfect scenario, as it gave him the opportunity to wear smart clothes and charm the ladies. He took the trouble to look suave in his midnight blue herringbone suit, double breasted as it was all the rage and he'd seen Cary Grant wearing one like it at the cinema. In those days of being young and single and before the onset of war, times seemed carefree and Vincent and his brothers had a lot of fun going to Blackpool with friends. This was a tradition in the North Country and on one of these jaunts his brother Maurice met a girl called Clara, whom he would eventually marry. Vincent was still very happy being unattached and as the years fell away he made the most of his youth.

Vincent aged 4 (1915).

Vincent and workmates from
D.P. Battery Co, early Thirties.

BLACKPOOL

Blackpool is a seaside town in Lancashire, which is part of a coastal plain situated between the Wyre and the Ribble with evidence of human existence back to the Palaeolithic Era. During Roman times the area was covered by dense oak forests. There are entries in the Domesday Book of the earliest villages on the plain and in medieval times the town was starting to emerge, as a few farms began to appear along the coast. The origins of the name are associated with a stream that drained a freshwater lake called Marton Mere and then ran through peat land, discolouring the water, hence *Blackpoole* which was first registered as an entry in 1602.

During the eighteenth century sea bathing was becoming en vogue for curing ailments, and wealthy visitors began visiting Blackpool. A private road was built in 1781 for easier access, and soon after a stage coach service began. In 1801, the town's population was listed as 473. Over the next few years the first holiday cottages were built and the arrival of the railways meant that Blackpool started to experience a steady influx of visitors, which gave the town the motivation for increasing its growth including new attractions. Soon the piers were completed, which made Blackpool the only town in the UK with three piers, and the Winter Gardens and Opera House were opened. The icing on Blackpool's cake would be the tower, which was completed in 1894 and gave the town a Parisian touch. Throughout the late 1800s the town continued to develop and this was intensified by the 'Wakes Weeks' where the cotton mills closed for a week every year in order for the factory owners to repair and service equipment. The workers were given this time as a holiday, and the focus became the seaside.

In a way Blackpool's character was founded on the town's use of electrical power. Electric street lighting was introduced in 1879, and although in the beginning it was just eight arc lamps, Blackpool's piece de resistance has become the illuminations, which today are a six-mile long light show which astounds visitors every year. Although over the years numbers may have dwindled and many might argue that British seaside towns (and Blackpool is no exception) have experienced their real heyday period, they retain a certain faded charm which is quite timeless.

Vincent spent most of the war years working for the D.P. Battery Company who were based in Bakewell, Derbyshire. Founded in Charlton, South London in 1888, the company moved to Bakewell in 1900. Vincent travelled around the country installing and servicing batteries in the large country houses of distinguished families, and as he did not drive a car these journeys were made by train or bus. The batteries were huge and extremely heavy so they were transported to different locations by a fleet of trucks. During the freezing winters he found himself stranded in all sorts of places.

For a time he was a regular guest at the Whermaccht Hotel where he introduced German prisoners to light ale, and often bought tobacco from a local town and sold it on at a profit. In late autumn one year he was sent on a job to a submarine in Plymouth and one of his jobs was to refill the batteries with acid. There were many dangers associated with the job and he accidentally spilt some acid that nearly overcame him, but luckily there was a member of staff there to help.

Vincent has fitted the batteries at Blenheim Palace and among the many places he stayed were Kilsby; Scarborough; Haythorne College; Melton Mowbray; Blackpool; Charlestown; Ullswater and Bakewell. A collection of postcards from these places enable him to remember this time in his life, and also to remember his future wife Ena, as he always sent her a postcard from every place he visited. Being a keen amateur photographer he always made sure he took his camera, and over the years Vincent has amassed a large and worthy photographic record of his family, travels and adventures.

Chewton Priory was a very grand country house that Vincent was assigned to work at. It nestled in the Mendip Hills in the Somerset village of Chewton Mendip. The house had a remarkable history. The family home of Lord and Lady Waldegrave, the house has hosted garden parties and visits from the gentry and many rich and famous characters of the Victorian era. The Waldegrave family had owned Chewton Mendip since 1553 but did not live in the village until the 1860s. Portraits of the family by Angelica Kauffman and Thomas Gainsborough hung in all their splendour in lofty rooms, but rather than be elevated by their aristocratic background they were a very balanced and down to earth family who were quite happy to provide food and board to a number of evacuees from London during the war. The beautiful Chewton Priory is no longer standing as it was taken down stone by stone and shipped to America.

It was on one of his visits to install the batteries that Vincent met Ena Church who was employed as a housekeeper at Chewton Priory, and it was her job to look after many of the noted people who came to stay. It was obvious straight away that she was sweet on him too, and they spent long balmy afternoons walking through Grigs Pit Valley, a long steep sided wooded ravine, with Vincent clasping her hand tight. One day he asked Ena to be his wife and she smiled as she took his hand in hers.

Vincent and Ena were married at the Weslyan Methodist Church on March 23rd 1940. Ena wore a dress of white satin and a veil and she carried a bouquet of red and white carnations. Lord and Lady Waldegrave both attended the ceremony and they gave a dinner service as a gift and all the staff at Chewton Priory gave Vincent and Ena a canteen of cutlery.

Vincent and Ena's first home was in Brislington near Bristol, which was the first house they rented as there were few mortgages in those days. Vincent was still working for the D.P. Company as this was a job that was considered helpful to the war effort, so it wasn't necessary for Vincent to join the forces. Before the children came along Ena often accompanied Vincent on his trips, and helped him to install the batteries. The one place they always went to together was a little town on the Devon coast called Sidmouth, that had seen a rise in popularity during the eighteenth & nineteenth centuries and had many attractive features including fine Georgian and Regency hotels. If they were feeling extravagant they stayed in one of the 'posh' hotels, otherwise it would be a nice bed and breakfast down by the seafront. Vincent remembers Ena describing how, having stayed behind one morning, she watched out of the window as prisoners were brought

Vincent refilling batteries, South Wales, late 1930s.

Vincent and Ena in Sidmouth, 1940.

Vincent and Ena's wedding day at Chewton Chapel, 1940.

Vincent and Ann, 1942.

Ena, Vincent and Bryan
relaxing in the grounds of
the Mendip Hospital, 1960.

down to the promenade and made to shovel pebbles. When his work was finished for the day they spent time together, sitting on a bench in Connaught Gardens as the sound of music carried from the bandstand, or strolling along the beach collecting red rocks that just might have fossils embedded in them.

During the war Ena was thrilled to discover that she was pregnant and in 1942 she gave birth to a baby girl that she christened Ann. Vincent adored his new baby daughter and adjusted to being a new father with ease. When Ann was two she remembers going to Bakewell with her mother and father. The town was founded by the Romans and is often seen as the gateway to the Peak District. Ann remembers the Victoria Mill, a huge water mill that ground corn until 1939, and how gigantic it had seemed. The family enjoyed strolling around the town and throwing bread for the ducks from the old bridge, which was built around 1300. They stayed with a lady called Mrs Peacock who used to take in lodgers, and the hallway she led you down was long and narrow with the smell of cigar smoke hanging in the air. Although they couldn't afford to stay there, the Rutland Hotel that looked over the main square in the town was the perfect place to stop for tea and as they sat savouring a slice of Bakewell Pudding, Vincent imagined the time that Jane Austen visited and perhaps wrote part of *Pride and Prejudice*.

The next move was to a hamlet in Chewton Mendip called Bathway, and a small thatched cottage called Chapel House. In 1948 Ena had her second child, a baby boy called Bryan, who was initially healthy and robust but was left profoundly deaf after contracting meningitis when he was 18 months old. Never to let his condition stop him having fun, when Bryan was two and playing a game of hide and seek, he hid under a bed with a lighted candle. As electricity had not been introduced to all households and candles was still the only source of light, Bryan had used the candle to guide his way in the darkness and had gone upstairs to find a good hiding place. The house caught fire and the whole family had to move out for a year, with Bryan staying with his grandmother whilst Ann had to go with whoever had room.

Vincent had always been very keen on photography and had made his own darkroom. He kept all the photographs in a teak box and when the house had caught fire it was the only thing he wanted to save. Taking all this into consideration there were many happy memories at Bathway. They had lots of hens and a wooden hen house that Vincent had made, and when the children were young they had a dog called Cherry. Vincent was very good at cutting hair and had a highly successful barber's business which he ran from the back garden. He often heard the sound of tapping coming from Tom Herard's next door as he hammered nails into wood, for Tom ran an undertaker's business and kept all the wood for making coffins in his shed.

During the 1950s all the previous travelling had taken its toll, and Vincent had found a new job at the Mendip Psychiatric Hospital in Wells. Built in Victorian times to Sir Gilbert Scott's striking design, this grade II listed building was home to the Bath and West County Asylum which was founded in 1848. Vincent was appointed to the role of head gardener and grounds-man and was to be responsible for the care and maintenance of the sports and recreation grounds, and 25 acres of ornamental gardens. He was very proud of his job and kept a ledger that had a record of his day to day duties and all the flowers and plants he had ordered … *Feb 3rd 1960 – 20 boxes of seeds sown, 3 boxes of Begonia and 3 boxes of Polyanthus; Feb 17th 1960 – 10 boxes of Dahlias.*

He travelled to work on a small motorbike until he bought his first car, and he was still driving until three years ago. The hospital felt that the job he was doing was essential, so the family were allocated Knapp Hill Farm which belonged to the hospital and was on the Bath Road in Wells. There were hydrangeas outside the front porch and they kept cows and pigs. Ena also had a job at the hospital working in the Occupational Therapy department. This part of the building had housed the isolation wards during the Polio outbreaks and each ward had row upon row of iron lungs.

Vincent worked in this position until his retirement in 1977 and they were then allocated a local authority bungalow in Wells, where they had lived ever since. Vincent's daughter Ann had married Norman and they also lived in Wells, and Berryman Court where Vincent and Ena lived was very close. They could literally walk down the steps at the bottom of the garden and across the railway line where the Strawberry Specials ran on summer evenings, with their ornate Victorian carriages and carry on up by the side of the rugby field, to Ann's back garden.

Vincent and Marianna (his 2nd great-granddaughter), 2001.

Vincent and Ena in the garden at Knapp Hill Farm, late 1960s.

Vincent and Ena used to walk along the railway track to feed the donkeys and he had always loved steam trains, especially the Coronation Scot prize train. This was a very special train which originated in 1937 for the Coronation of King George VI. He had seen it once before and it was in service until the start of the war in 1939, running between London and Glasgow.

Vincent and Ena had a lot of good times and would go on many adventures. When they were feeling nostalgic they went to Sidmouth or for long walks on the Mendip Hills, and once they ventured further and went to London and visited the Barbican. Vincent's favourite place was the city of Bath and after Ena passed away in July 2000 she was cremated at Bath Crematorium, with her ashes scattered at Chewton Priory in the position where they originally met.

After Ann lost her mother she became concerned about her father and how he would cope without her. They had been a team for so long that she felt he may struggle emotionally. The last ten years have not been easy but it has been a godsend living so close to each other. On many occasions Ann might pop in to visit her father to find the house empty, as Vincent had got on a train and gone to Bath. A place of great beauty and serenity, the Romans had established Bath as a spa resort in AD43 and it became extremely popular during the Georgian Era. Just wandering the city was an enjoyable pastime, and he would start by taking breakfast at the Pump Rooms and then go on to see the changing themes at the Parade Gardens. This was always a very special place as he and Ena had often taken the Harrison Riverside path, imagining the society folk of the day strolling along the promenade. These popular pleasure gardens that overlook the River Avon were originally an orchard that belonged to the Abbey and the floral displays are beautiful, especially the summer features. Concerts are frequently held on warm afternoons and they often sat and listened to the loose notes that hung in the air.

These memories are what brighten Vincent's days as he now resides at Frith House.

ELIZABETH 'BESSIE' BARNES

*'My dreams are forever lasting and live in my past.
I'm going through things and I don't want to forget.'*

BESSIE WAS BORN on November 10th 1910 in Pontypridd, which is 12 miles from Cardiff between the Rhondda and Taff valleys. Bessie's father Sam had travelled from Weston Super Mare looking for a job in the coal mines. Her mother Matilda was from Neath and had long red Titian hair. She was well known for helping her friends and neighbours when they went into labour. The couple met when Sam was lodging with Matilda's aunt and he met the beautiful flame-haired girl when she went to visit the family.

D.O.B. 10/11/1910

Bessie was the seventh of eight children although before she was born her mother had lost two sons who died, with her father buying a burial plot for the ashes. Bessie was born on the Graig at a time when they were building many new houses on the mountains. Pontypridd was a mining town and an important location for transporting coal from the Rhondda via the Glamorganshire canal and then the Taff Vale Railway, which is one of the oldest in Wales. Life revolved around the collieries and when her brothers grew up they went to work in the pits, even though they didn't like it. The dangers of the mines were accepted but when Bessie's eldest brother Sam joined the Army it nearly broke her mother's heart. During her childhood the long lonely journey into the darkness of the mines was a way of life and a necessity for the men and Bessie would watch as her father set off for work with his Tommy box full of cheese, carrying a jack which had cold tea in it.

When she was old enough to start school Bessie can remember being led by the hand as her sisters took her to the building where the infants were taught. There was a row of tin buildings, one for the infants and a separate one for the girls and boys and there were open fires to warm the rooms and an abundance of fuel, as most of the men were working in the pits. Coal was an inexpensive fuel and was delivered by horse and cart along roads that were still rough and earthy. Bessie remembers the men building the roads and all the children getting very muddy on their way to school in the morning.

Just before the First World War began people had started to emigrate to Canada, as they knew there was going to be a war. The men went first to secure jobs but when war broke out they were brought back to fight and the women were left behind. After the war the men returned to Canada, which is how Bessie's aunt and uncle started their new life. During the war the country was desperate for coal to make ammunitions but in the heart of rural Wales there was little experience of German bombardment and the people were generally unaffected by the conflict.

At school Bessie liked doing maths. The English teacher Miss John lived fairly close and also taught Welsh as it was the natural dialect, so Bessie has gone through her life speaking both languages. The headteacher Miss Spraggen was very strict and if you were late she made you hold your hand out for the cane. In the morning Bessie had two rounds of toast and margarine for breakfast and at lunchtime Auntie Nelly who lived across the road would come to the gates to pass buttered bread and jam and a carton of milk through the railings. Bessie's parents had always been friends with the James family who ran the dairy and Matilda would get free milk, and in return Bessie often went and did the washing up as Mrs James had many children to look after.

Bessie left school when she was 14, and for the next three years she worked in the nearby Woolworths store and helped out at the local dairy. She and her brother Tommy were very close and both loved jazz music, and once they swapped clothes and went to a fancy dress party with Bessie dressed in a very smart brown woollen suit. There was always something to laugh about and she was a natural extrovert who loved to have fun. This happy go lucky nature was sure to attract attention before long.

Bessie had noticed Harry Barnes around as he lived nearby and had always been friendly with her brother. One evening after a night out with friends she came home to find him sitting at the kitchen table, drinking tea. Harry was a lovely dancer and was almost semi-professional and had just returned from Cardiff, where he and his partner had won a Waltz Competition. Harry had been so happy and proud that he had a couple of drinks. Feeling slightly giddy he had knocked on the back door and said to Bessie's brother "If I go home now my father will kill me" so stayed to try and sober himself up. He had grinned at Bessie when she walked through the door that evening and later he told her brother that he would marry her one day. From this point on Harry always took the long way round so that he could walk past her house. He adored her parents, calling them Ma and Pa, and was always at her house playing cards with his feet up on a chair.

The problem with all this attention from Harry Barnes was that Bessie was already going out with another man, Jim. They had been courting for a few months but Jim knew something wasn't quite right and when they said goodnight on her doorstep, he would say, "I know Harry Barnes is in there … well Harry Barnes don't make any difference to me". Bessie knew that she had to get away to think about things and get over these two boys. After a very busy festive season Woolworths had started to make their staff redundant so Bessie asked her mother if she could go and stay with her Aunt Lizzie in Neath and look for another job. However after a few weeks she realised there were even fewer jobs in Neath so decided to return home. As the train pulled in to the station, Harry Barnes was standing on the platform. In Bessie's words, "that kiss said it all". Bessie felt older and more in control. As they walked home she noticed Jim standing at a bus stop but she knew she was going home with Harry. Before they had even reached her front door, he had asked her to marry him.

August 3rd 1929 was a beautiful summer day. As the church was within walking distance, Bessie and Harry's wedding procession made a pretty picture with the smallest girls carrying armfuls of fresh flowers. Her eldest sister Nelly had sent her some ivory satin and another sister, May, who was a tailoress, had made her a beautiful dress. Her father gave her away and welcomed Harry into the family with a broad smile, and it seemed that the whole town had come out to celebrate. They spent their wedding night in a hotel in Bristol, which was a gift from one of Harry's brothers, and then

Harry and Bessie.

started married life with his parents in Pontypridd until they found a house of their own. Before long a mutual friend put them in touch with an elderly lady who was living alone in a large house in town and needed help, so Bessie and Harry were offered the house-rent free.

Bessie didn't have a job as women didn't generally work after they were married, and there wasn't really enough work for married women anyway. Harry was lucky to have had the opportunity to learn a trade, and through help and support from his family he raised £100 for his apprenticeship and became a fully-qualified electrician. Most homes still had no electricity and he worked inside the tram-car depots as a maintenance man, but when he lost his job they decided to move away as there was a better chance of a job in Somerset.

When Bessie moved to Yeovil in 1936 she was eight months pregnant and had planned to call the baby Sylvane if it was a girl, having read the name in a novel and liked it. She found a very good doctor called Dr Gower and when he was called up during the Second World War his wife took his place, and remained her doctor for years. When Harry and Bessie first arrived in Yeovil they stayed with Harry's brother, where initially you had to put a penny in the slot for gaslight and there was a coal fire that you could fit a sturdy pot over. Things were very hard at first while Harry looked for work and when her baby daughter was born the cost of her birth certificate was sixpence, which was all the money they had. They moved into their first house at 2 Marl Close in 1937 and Bessie had her second child Eric, both children being fairly easy home births. Harry had found a job with the Westland Aviation Company, which was seen as a reserve occupation when war broke out. There had already been rumours of an impending war, especially from Westland, who were making aeroplanes for the future war effort.

Life was difficult during the war. If you had children you were entitled to slightly more rations so there was extra milk and eggs. Bessie had her third child, Ken, on June 3rd 1941, giving birth to him in a makeshift hospital on the Ilchester Road while Bessie's sister looked after the other two children. The house was heated by a coal fire and there was no hot water so all water had to be boiled, and there was still no electricity so candles and portable gaslights were used. Bessie saw very little of Harry as he would come home from work, have his supper and have a rest before going out during the night with the Home Guard, to check windows for blackout curtains and make sure the roads were in good repair. Bessie's mother had already passed away but her father and youngest sister were living with her so she wasn't alone during the night with the children.

Yeovil had become one of Britain's main centres of aircraft defence industries which made it a frequent target for enemy bombers. The worst of the bombing was during 1940 and 1942 when 107 high explosive bombs fell on Yeovil, killing 49 people and causing serious damage to over 3,000 homes. On one occasion an American airbase was bombed and a line of planes were seen strafing with their machine guns down the main street in Yeovil. The main targets though were the airport and Westland.

Bessie and Harry in the front garden of Milford Road, 1960s.

WESTLAND

Westland is a British aircraft manufacturer located in Yeovil. It was founded in 1915 by J.P. Petter & Sons who had made petrol and diesel engines since 1896. They had also built the first internal combustion engine motor car to be made in the UK. In 1915 Westland Aircraft

Works was established in response to a call from the government for certain aircraft and in the last years of the First World War, the Westland N.1B, the Wagtail and the Weasel were created.

During World War II, Westland designed the Whirlwind, a twin-engined dual cannon fighter which was a contemporary of the Hawker Hurricane and was one of Britain's fastest aircraft. However problems arose with the constant delay of its Rolls Royce Peregrine engines and only a few were built. Westland also built the Lysander, an intermediary aircraft that was involved in many covert operations, initially message dropping and artillery spotting. Small unprepared airstrips were adequate as the Lysander only needed a short take off. They were easy targets for the Luftwaffe though and were withdrawn during the Dunkirk evacuation.

After the war Westland focused more on helicopters and signed an agreement with Sikorsky, an American aircraft company founded in 1925, which developed the first secure single rotor helicopter and is responsible for the UH 60 Black Hawk. Many mergers took place between the companies between 1953 and 1960 and in 1961, Westland Helicopters was born. In 1986 a political crisis engulfed Westland, resulting in the resignation of Conservative Minister Michael Heseltine. In 2000 the company merged with the Italian syndicate, Augusta.

In the aftermath of war people did their best to reach a semblance of normality. The first school that Ken went to was on Stiby Road and he would remember this building in years to come when it was time for his mother to move out of the bungalow. In the early years after the war council houses were being made of concrete rather than brick, as the country was desperate to rebuild and concrete was a cheaper commodity. There was no electricity initially in Yeovil but now the council were building houses and putting in three lights and a plug. As he was an electrician Harry had plenty of work so the family were quite comfortable, and an opportunity arose for the family to move into one of the new houses on Milford Road.

The realisation that she did not have her own personal finances hit Bessie one day when she was asking Harry for the children's pocket money and she thought, "It's time I got a job". She knew just the kind of job she wanted. Yeovil had been at the centre of the glove making industry since the 1800s. These businesses had helped the town expand and by the 1830s it was said that three million pairs were made each year. There were factories all over town and Bessie secured a job with the Goldcroft factory. She made friends with Ann Yates, who when not at work could always be found in the Catholic church on Lonsdale Road. The gloving industry started from the leather and the skins which were made at the Pittard factory on Sherbourne Road, where the leather was tanned and prepared, ready for the cutters and stitchers. The first floor of Goldcroft's was where all the leather and linings came in and it was sorted into different grades and on the next floor there were rows of machines where the ladies put the linings in the gloves. Bessie also did a bit of glove making at home as there were many jobs for outworkers. There weren't many houses in Yeovil which didn't have a gloving machine but if you didn't have one you did it by hand, numbering or putting the gloves in pairs or making linings. This was how the women of Yeovil lived and you were paid for what you did, earning up to £3 a week.

Bessie always missed her homeland and the importance of place within society was apparent for her, as she noticed a certain prejudice that was directed at the Welsh people. Harry sometimes

Sylvane and Bessie,
July 1956.

experienced it at Westlands as many of the English felt that the Welsh had taken their jobs. Many years ago, groups of Welsh people seeking work had walked from Swansea to Yeovil in search of a better life and Bessie would encounter these people when she worked for the St John's Ambulance as a volunteer. There was a stone workhouse locally where elderly people went if they needed shelter and support, and many of the Welsh who migrated to Somerset ended up there. Bessie sympathised with these people and realised how lucky she was, and would often relieve the nurses so they could have a break. One way she managed to keep her Welsh roots alive was by singing in the choir, and she did this for many years in church halls and community centres.

Over the years the children made their own way in life and it wasn't long before they had flown the nest. Sylvane's face was badly scarred in a car accident and she was awarded compensation. The insurance company decided that the money should be put toward her education, so she got a scholarship and trained in shorthand typing at West Bay College. Whilst there she met her first husband through a friend and they emigrated to Canada. Eric's girlfriend was a telephonist called Louise but at 19 he was soon to do his National Service. Ken was a teenager and had a part-time job on the *Western Gazette* but Sylvane had encouraged him to go to Canada where there were many jobs on local papers. When he was old enough to stand on his own feet he followed her advice and flew to North America.

The winter of 1960 was one of the worst Britain had experienced for years but as Christmas approached the festive season took hold and the sight of snow on the ground was beautiful. Ken had been back in Yeovil for a few months and had found a job working for the Yeovil Timber Company. As Christmas was a costly affair he had a part-time job on the trading estate, working for a friend who had a garage and sold tyres. He was dressed up ready for a Christmas party and had a date with a girl from Yeovil hospital. Just as he was about to leave he got a phone call from his boss, asking him to go and deliver some snow tyres to a regular customer in Bridgwater. The snow was everywhere and it was getting worse but he agreed as he didn't like to let his friend down. His car overturned on an icy road and he was trapped underneath and the ambulance men

Eric in uniform doing National Service, 1960s.

Right: Bessie wearing a blouse she made with Sylvane, Harry and baby.

Far right: Bessie, Harry, Sylvane, Jeffrey and the girls in America.

Harry and Bessie in America.

had to drag him out. Ken had broken his spine and was left paralysed, and has been in a wheelchair ever since.

Bessie visited her daughter regularly in North America, proudly showing off her plane tickets at work. Sylvane had divorced her first husband and married an American called Jeffrey who was in television during its heyday and was fairly wealthy. Initially Harry drove Bessie to Heathrow Airport, choosing to stay behind as he didn't like the thought of flying, but once he had got over his fear of flying he couldn't visit enough and loved the country. After he retired he went to Canada to build a fence for Sylvane and Jeffrey and when he came back there was a very expensive car waiting for him at the docks as a thank you present. When they weren't flying across the world Bessie and Harry spent a lot of holidays in North Wales and the Lake District and they celebrated their Golden Wedding anniversary with a big party that was held in the community centre.

Bessie proudly says that she had a good marriage and she loved Harry Barnes with all her heart. He was always an appreciative husband and she remembers once when she was going out to bingo and had made herself a dress. As she smoothed herself down in front of the mirror she

Far left: Harry and Bessie in the Lake District.

Left: Harry and Bessie on their Golden Wedding anniversary.

Bessie sitting contemplating.

turned to him and said, "Do I look alright?" He hadn't been feeling very well and was sitting by the fire and he said "Of course you do!" Bessie said, "No really, I'm talking sense now!" and Harry said "You always look nice to me". She turned to him and said "How can I look nice if I'm about s eventy?!" but in her heart she knew she'd made the right choice all those years ago.

After Harry passed away, Bessie continued to live on her own in the bungalow. Her children are there for her whenever she needs them. She lost her son Eric after a long illness and Sylvane visits from America when she can. Ken has been a dedicated son who always remembers her birthday and does wonderful things for her. One day Ken came to visit and said "I want you to come with me!" and he took her to see Lockwood Court. It was the place he first went to school, which had recently been turned into a sheltered housing block but was still unoccupied. The garden was beautiful but there was one snag, which was the distance from the front door. Ken said, "If you like the flat you can have it and we'll take care of you". Bessie has been at Lockwood Court now for nearly twenty years and is fairly happy although sometimes it can be lonely. She was one of the first residents to move in and at the time there was a full time warden called Pauline, who was permanently on call and cooked lovely meals. She and another lady called Barbara would take her out and the atmosphere was jolly. Over the years Lockwood Court has changed and altered and everything thinned down until just the tenants remained. Now there are temporary scheme managers and Bessie is taken to the hospital or surgery if necessary and Somerset Care At Home are always on call. Bessie is very good friends with several of her neighbours and has just had a fabulous party to celebrate her 100th birthday, with friends and family coming from North America and Wales.

EVE MONKTON

*'From my window I can look out and see the orchard,
and smell Ben Mitchell's beef roasting in the oven'*

D.O.B. 21/12/1907

EVE WAS BORN on December 21st 1907 in the Somerset village of Merriot. Her father Bertram Pattermore built a new brick house on Bake House Corner as a family home. Eve's mother was called Bertha England and she came from an accounting family who had several holidays a year. She turned the front parlour into a shop and sold provisions and groceries to the local community. As well as being a builder Eve's father was a carpenter and wheelwright, repairing wheels for carts and wagons. During the First World War he had to make so many gun carriage wheels that he had a bad back for months. He had a workshop in the orchard and kept his father's prize cattle in the adjoining field, and Eve still remembers the night when he had a terrible argument with her grandfather over a valuable cow that died after a hard pear got stuck in its windpipe.

The Pattermores had horses on their farm and when the war broke out the war department commandeered four of the horses for the war effort. They only took two shires in the end, including Blossom, who was Eve's favourite. She had stayed up for long nights when Blossom's leg was injured and had often been woken by the mare kicking the stable door. It was very much a family affair and the Englands and Pattermores were a good team. Her eldest uncle milked the cows, Uncle Sam grew crops, and everyone had their place. Eve was the eldest of five and her youngest sister Mary wasn't a very strong child, becoming ill during the flu epidemic of 1918-1922. When she recovered a little dog was bought for her, which she named Bonzo and which followed her everywhere.

The children were not allowed out on the streets and were never given a piece of bread and jam to eat outside, as their mother said that, "the table is the place for food". When Eve was nine she was bought a doll's pram as a special treat and arranged her perfectly dressed dolls in a line, sometimes tucking her teddy bear in between. During the winter the children had to come straight home from school, and as there was no gas or electricity Eve was in charge of lighting the lamps. There was one lamp for the living room and another for the grocer's shop and her father showed her how to light them using petrol, teaching her to be very careful and push the wick in slowly.

Whilst at Merriot School Eve was good at 'reckoning' (maths) but bad at spelling, and she was given the cane one day by the headmaster because she spelt the word 'biscuit' incorrectly. Her father was furious and went to the school and caught hold of Johnny Paplin by the neck, saying," If you hit my daughter again, you will have the same and don't forget it". Eve's hand was so sore that she

Eve in approximately 1912.

Eve's wedding day on
Christmas Day, 1933.

couldn't grip anything for days.

Eve used to attend cookery lessons in Crewkerne and one day the children made chocolate pudding, which Eve's mother said was like a door-stopper because it was so hard. One day the children were having drill and Mr Barlow came running out into the playground and said "Children!! Children!! The war is over!!" The children ran home and people were streaming out of the factory in jubilation and Eve remembers her father being in bed with the flu but still hugging her mother tight.

Eve's grandparents were tailors and they worked together in a little room over the main bar in the Kings Head pub. Customers could often hear the whirr of the sewing machine as they sipped their stout. They lived in a house in the village and people came with brown paper packages of 'cheap' stuff from abroad, asking them to make a suit or trousers. The villagers came together on a Sunday as Ben Mitchell the baker cooked the 'Sunday Bake'. As his ovens were so large people would give him a joint of meat and a tray of potatoes and pay him to cook the meals for the entire village. Bessie's father had a car and he cut the bodywork up and turned it into a truck so he could take the dinners around the village. The first car that Bertram Pattermore ever bought was an early Model T Ford, and when Eve was thirteen he let her drive to the Kings Heads to pick someone up with Uncle Jack in tow. Bertram had bought the car from a doctor who lived at Egwood Farm, which was on the crossroads through the forest, and he started a taxi business and would transport people to Weymouth for a few pennies.

When Eve left school she helped her mother around the house, although Bertha had employed a woman who came to clean the bedrooms every Thursday. She washed the linoleum floor and polished it when it was dry. Bertha always cleaned the grate though she felt nobody else did it to the right standard. Most of the groceries were obtained from the Bake House shop but if they ran out of cheese Eve cycled to Crewkerne or took the Petherton (which was very cheap) and went to Nicholls where they cut the pork belly by hand into thick rashers of bacon. She put the money in her underwear and fastened it with a safety pin to make sure she didn't lose it. Eve always looked forward to the annual church choir outing to Lyme Regis where everyone had a free tea and there was a nice shop down by the seafront where she always bought a little brooch or keepsake, and sometimes a posy of dried flowers for her mother.

When Eve was fifteen she was recommended by her Aunt Kay to help run a grocer's shop for a friend whose eldest daughter was getting married, so she left home and went to Bournemouth. This was to be a very happy part of her life. She worked hard behind the counter taking orders and would weigh out sugar, wrap cold pats of butter, and gently place small brown eggs in paper bags. She wasn't lonely as her cousin lived locally and she had made great friends with the manager's daughter, and they would go down to the seafront or cycle down to Allum Chime, staying out of the way of the train tracks. This steep river valley led onto wonderful sandy beaches or you could walk through the woods to Westbourne. She particularly loved the Tropical gardens and taking the zig-zag path across the cliff tops to look out across Poole Bay.

If they were in the town they sometimes went into an upmarket tea shop called Boveys, which had a baby grand piano where a lady would play Brahms. When the bill came they had just enough money to pay and then they would go to the Westbourne Cinema and sit with the children as the tickets were cheap - if the auditorium filled up they would be asked to move. At the time the films were silent and a lady would play the piano in a sunken area, hitting the keys hard when something exciting happened. Uncle Harry would meet them to walk them home, as they had to pass an area where the boats came in and it would be dark.

THE GENIUS OF BRAHMS

The German pianist and composer Johannes Brahms was born on May 7th 1833 in Hamburg and is one of the masters of the Romantic Era. As a boy his time was devoted to reading and composing music, and he developed a love for folklore including poems, tales and music. He was a zealous worker and took inspiration from all around, compiling a book of English folk songs in his teens and later, in 1852, influenced by a poem by Count Kraft Von Toggenburg, he wrote the F sharp Piano Sonata op.2.

Brahms settled in Vienna and was seen by some as the obvious successor to Beethoven. His blend of classicism with its romantic expression and harmony put him in opposition to the more volatile aggressive musical style of Wagner and Liszt.

Brahms' complete oeuvre is quite breathtaking. He wrote four massive symphonies, completed some two dozen pieces of chamber music, sumptuous piano sonatas and the famous Hungarian Dances. Brahms' collection of music also includes a large number of songs including the charming Wiegenlied (Cradle Song). The beauty of Brahms' outstanding repertoire is that it makes 'musical sense' which has to be the highest accolade a composer can be awarded.

When Eve was twenty-one she had to return home as her mother had another child, Mary, whom Eve had to help look after her. Christmas was approaching, and the snow was deep. It was Christmas Eve and her mother had shut the shop at six o'clock as they were to travelling to Temple Combe by pony and trap with Lily and baby Mary. They were going to visit some friends that Bertram worked for and on the way they stopped for a hot toddy which gave the pony a chance to rest. They carried on for another sixteen miles in the freezing cold although everyone was wrapped up snugly with a leather cover pulled over their knees, which covered the baby as well. When they arrived Uncle Alf carried Lily in and the men took themselves off to smoke their pipes. The stars were bright and Sam nearly skidded down the icy path.

Bertram Pattermore was a master carpenter, and when he had made a new wagon he sent it to Blake's in Crewkerne for painting. A poster on the oak tree in the village was advertising the services of a painter at half the normal price and this was how Eve met her husband, William, who was learning his trade. He did a fine job on the wagon, as he knew if you learnt your trade well you would succeed as there was no time for a bad craftsman.

Eve and William were married at Merriot Church by Reverend Percival on Christmas Day 1933, and she wore a shiny blue silk dress and a veil. After they were married they lived in Ox Elms, the same house that her father built. William was working as a painter and had a three-year apprenticeship earning five shillings a week. Eve was working as a glove maker although she didn't earn much as she was quite slow. After a while she changed jobs and started to make the big hard cuffs for pilots' gloves and her wages increased. There were three glove manufacturers in the area and they were all competing for trade and a good workforce.

Eve had her first child, Peter, in 1937. She had been expecting twins but the farmer's dog had

A stroll on Weymouth seafront, late 1930s. *Left to right:* Eve's husband Billy, Eve, Eve's mother Bertha Pattermore and father Bert.

Local friend's wedding day, Eve is 3rd from left and Peter is the child (front right).

Late Thirties in Weymouth.

Eve, Jean and Rachael taking a stroll at Stourhead, Wiltshire 1988.

jumped up at her and she had lost one of the babies, a perfect little girl. When Eve had felt the first pangs of labour she had cycled to her mother's house in Merriot and between her and nurse Patterson they helped Eve with the birth. There had been birthing meetings but she hadn't gone to all of them as she felt she had lots of experience being the eldest.

Eve had a marvellous district nurse called Miss Judd who was one of the best, and Peter was a good baby. Eve only lost sleep when he was teething and then she and William took it in turns to get up and see to him. Peter was two when the war broke out.

During the war many young women had to go and work in ammunition factories, as the men were away. William was working in a hospital in Axminster that housed many wounded American soldiers and he would leave for work at 5 o'clock in the morning, cycle to the station and catch the train. He was away for the week working on the buildings and repairing the war damage, coming home at the weekends. During this time soldiers were billeted in Stoke Sub Hamden, including many Americans, although Eve had two young men from Devon staying with her. The adjacent field was full of army machinery and tanks, jeeps and lorries always blocked the lane outside the house. A guard called Leroy Bates was patrolling the garage and he sat in a chair on the garage forecourt, a big machine gun hanging by his side, and he would stare straight at people passing by with heavy eyes. Peter remembers him carving his name in beautiful curved letters on some wooden rails across the road but unfortunately Tom Lord's pony bolted one day and made the man who drove the marmalade lorry swerve and crash into Leroy Bates' fine work.

There were many soldiers around in the build-up to D-Day. Eve can remember the day that a German bomber came through Stoke at roof-top level, as they could beat the radar if they flew under fifty feet high. The bomber was heading for Crewkerne and went straight over the house and she could actually see the pilot and pushed Peter under the stone draining board in the scullery. They bombed a local dairy and on a moonlit night, the reflection of the moon of the greenhouses was thought to be like the moon on water and a possible target. Peter can remember collecting squares of silver foil from the fields that the Germans used to drop from planes as another way of beating the radar. Certain local airfields and buildings were seen as viable targets and there was supposedly a secret location in Westonzoyland.

Hampden Hall was the place to go if you wanted to let your hair down and have some fun. The Americans would often organise dances and ply all the pretty girls with silk stockings, which were a luxury. Eve was married by this point so there was no danger of her falling for the charms of an American but when she was a girl her father would threaten her with the Chard Union (a home for unmarried mothers), telling her she'd be sent there if she got into any trouble. This was enough encouragement to make a young girl keep any chap at arms length.

The shortages during the war were difficult for most families. As the ration for petrol was three gallons a month William left his car in the garage most of the time, and they kept chickens and grew their own vegetables, which helped a little. Eve used to do all the glove machining by day and shearing by night, as William didn't want the machine going at night.

Sherman tanks lined the road and Peter named his hand-cart 'hot rock' after his favourite tank. He was best friends with Colin Welsh who lived in Fourwinds, a house along the street, and they would take 'hot rock' to the top of the hill at dusk, with Peter holding a box aloft, containing a jam jar with a candle in it as Colin pushed. Colin also had a 'cat's whisker' which was a made-

Far left: Even and Eva Welsh (Billy's's sister) - they used to get along so well, they were like sisters, 1990s.

Left: 100th birthday celebration in 2007 at Peter's house with Peter, his wife Jean and granddaughters Rachael and Velda.

up radio with a crystal and a little wire on the end of a lever on which you could hear the BBC if you pushed it onto the crystal.

After the war things became a little easier, although many shortages continued into the 1950s and the country was scarred with war damage. If they had enough petrol William would get the car out and they would all drive to the seaside, visiting West Bay or Lyme Regis. When Peter was fifteen he was in isolation at Petherton Hospital with suspected polio after collapsing on his paper round. The booming voice of Dr Powers Fox assured Eve that he would be fine, and he was prescribed medicines and potions. There were eight patients to each ward with a nurse to each one and there were no pillows. It wasn't long before Peter made a full recovery and returned home.

Eve continued to make gloves at home for the Percombe factory, and she also worked all day on Tuesdays and Fridays in a hardware shop in Stoke. Occasionally she also worked in a fruit shop in Yeovil, travelling to work with William as he had a painting job in town. Peter went into the Royal Air Force in 1957, and in 1963 he married his childhood sweetheart Jean and moved into a house nearby, following in his grandfather's footsteps and setting himself up in business as a builder.

William retired in 1968 and they now spent any free time together. Gardening was a passion that Eve and William had always shared, and they grew six-foot high dahlias and had beautiful flowerbeds bordering the house. Eve kept the lawn immaculate and she used to cut it with a petrol mower, the plugs of which William ensured were all covered and clean. After William retired they managed to live on their weekly pensions and they had always been careful, making sure there was a pound or two on the sideboard. Eve would often walk up the street to the local village shop, or sometimes catch the free bus to the Asda supermarket.

It was very difficult for Eve when William passed away and before he left her he said, "I wish we could go on together … I don't want to leave you behind". Eve is still living alone and Peter does everything he can to help his mother, visiting her every couple of days. For the last two years carers have been coming to help Eve but she is fiercely independent and would complain when they tried to put her to bed. As she has become more fragile and has suffered the occasional fall and bad cold, the carers now come four or five times a day. The familiarity of her own home is so important and she is able to continue to live in her own home because of the care she receives. From the bay window she can look out at the fields and see the orchard, and sometimes even still smells Ben Mitchell's beef roasting in the oven.

At Yeovil Church for the wedding of granddaughter Velda, 1992.

HAROLD DARE

'I'm living as good a life as I can!'

D.O.B. 14/08/1911

HAROLD WAS BORN in 1911 in a part of West Lyng in Somerset known as Outwood. He grew up in a cottage alongside Durston railway station in this small hamlet and his father George Henry worked on the railways all his life, fixing the 'permanent way', which were the tracks that consisted of rails, sleepers and ballast. Most of the men in the area worked on the railways and they would walk or cycle to work. Harold had three brothers and five sisters, and when he was just five one of his brothers died in the nearby Taunton and Bridgwater Canal. From then on none of the children were allowed to go near the water and he never learnt to swim. Harold's eldest sister Elsie had found employment in London where she was in service, and she later met her husband there, who was serving in the Coldstream Guards.

Harold is very proud to say that he and his siblings were all brought up properly and were taught to treat people well. The family lived in a three bedroomed cottage, which still exists today. Harold went to the village school, which was a mile's walk away, and sometimes he spun his hoop as he walked, using a crook that the village blacksmith had made. There was no traffic on the roads in those days so it was quite safe to use the country lanes. The school was a two-roomed building close to the village of East Lyng and educated children between 5 and 14. Harold was not overly keen on school but his teacher Miss Jordan thought he was an angelic boy and treated him like the teacher's pet.

When Harold was 14 he left school and went to work at David Greggs, a provisions merchant. Groceries were sold on one side of the shop and meat, bacon and cheese on the other. He was just biding time as what he really wanted to do was become a precision engineer, but he had to wait until he was 16 before he could begin an apprenticeship. He signed a 5-year contract with W.F. Wills, an engineering company in Bridgwater, and cycled in all weathers from Outwood, as a bicycle was the only thing he could afford. All workers had to arrive on time as the foreman blew the whistle on the stroke of nine and then walked out to the big iron gates and pulled them shut. If you were late you were not allowed through the gates and would lose a day's pay. The end of the day was announced once again by the whistle, at which time the men would put down their tools and make their way home. When his apprenticeship was complete he found a job working for an engineering company in Chippenham, travelling there by motorbike. He found himself rooms in a lodging house and went home to visit his family at the weekend.

When Harold wasn't working there were plenty of ways to have fun. The local village hall in Durston hosted a dance on most Saturday nights where a five piece band usually played. Harold

Harold and Doris'
Wedding Day, 1939.

The evacuees - Bob,
Doris, little Daphne
and John, 1940.

was quite a hit with the ladies and they thought he was a terrific dancer.   He was a popular young man and enjoyed socialising with a wide circle of friends.   He was particularly friendly with the sons of a local farmer in Creech Heathfield and they often rode their motorcycles together, and he would call by on the way to a dance.   The daughters and their girl-friends would usually be sitting round the kitchen table looking at nylons or lipstick in a copy of *Cosmopolitan* or *Ladies Home Journal*.   There was one girl that Harold recognised sitting at the table one Saturday evening.   Her name was Doris and she drove a pony and trap around the local villages delivering oil, measured by the gallon and used for lighting, cooking and heating.   Harold and Doris hit it off straight away.   After they had courted for some time, he pledged his troth to Doris and one of the farmer's daughters whispered, "I wish you'd waited a bit longer for me!" but Harold knew he'd met the girl he was going to marry.

Just after the war started Harold and Doris were married in Creech St Michael church on September 23rd 1939.   They continued to live in Outwood in the house next door to the one he had grown up in.   Ron and Miriam Lane moved in to Harold's old house soon afterwards and they all became great friends, although Harold always addressed Miriam as 'Mrs Lane' as he had old-fashioned values and felt it more courteous.   Soon after the war there was a new addition to the Lane family when Miriam gave birth to a baby daughter, Beryl.   Over the years the two families became close and Doris and Miriam often went to whist drives together whilst Harold looked after Beryl, and when she got older they listened to 'Top of the Form' on the radio and cheered when the team they were supporting won.

When Harold got married he was working as a precision engineer for a small family business in Street.   He was very happy in his work and had no desire to leave.   But things were going to change, as there were certain rules for the direction of labour expected for the war effort.   One day Harold received a telephone call from the labour exchange in Street and was informed that he had to leave his job and go to a new one.   He had two options: one was a job in the north of England (which didn't appeal to Harold, as he was a Somerset man and the north seemed like another country); and the other was to work for a company in Taunton, located at the bottom of Fore Street.   Harold felt a little suspicious as he knew this company were motor engineers and had probably the biggest motor showroom in Taunton, but he didn't know a thing about motor engineering.   Harold had a meeting with a man called Mr Edwards who drove him to the works building on the Wellington Road and showed him into a small workshop.   Harold was still very curious so the man explained.

As Britain was at war it seemed the company was going to help maintain RAF aircraft and they wanted to set up a munitions department, employing a team of women to replace the men who had been called up for the war effort.   They already had one person from London running a shift but needed someone to run the other.   When Harold returned to Doris' parents' house at Creech Heathfield to meet Doris, she asked him if he had the job and his mother in law exclaimed, "Of course he got the job! You know they couldn't refuse him".

So it was that Harold became a shift supervisor for Marshalsea's Hydraulics.   On his first day of work he met the chairman of the company, a suave London businessman called Bennett who looked him up and down and said, "Do you know anything?"   Harold felt slightly taken aback but replied, "Well if I don't then what am I here for?!"   It was Harold's job to run day and night shifts, alternating with a man called Frank Dominy.   There were sixteen girls in total and they all turned out to be excellent workers, instilling a camaraderie in the workplace that Harold had never experienced before.

The experience of war in Somerset was totally unlike that of London. Although it was frightening when the Germans dropped bombs in the country it was quite a rarity, and all the children wanted to take a look at the crater that had been made. It was a different story in the big cities with the bombing particularly bad in London, causing many children to be sent away to the country. During the war Harold and Doris took in many evacuees and Harold will never forget the look on the boys' faces that resembled haunted animals. Every day Doris cycled to Creech Heathfield and did whatever she had to do for her mother before returning home to her new family. She wouldn't turn any child away and if anyone came along telling tales about one of the children she would say, "No! No! No! Not one of my boys", defending them against all the odds. These young lads would always be 'her boys'. It seemed like a rural idyll to these children, and having the expanse of fields and woods on their doorstep was a joy. They also loved to play on the canal that cut through the fields behind the cottages, although it unnerved Harold after losing his brother as a child. A commemorative bench has been placed there now as a way of thanking the Dares for everything they did.

Bob and John, 1940.

Bob, Freddie and John, 1941.

OPERATION PIED PIPER

As early as 1924 and after the horrors of the First World War, the logistics of mass evacuation were being planned and a committee was set up to organise the movement of people to a safer place. As Britain's cities were to be targets of German bombing raids during the Second World War mass evacuation would take place, and children were to be sent to the country for safety. This was to be one of the biggest social upheavals the country had ever seen. For some it was to be a traumatic experience and for others a great adventure. At 11.07 on Thursday 31st August 1939 the order to 'evacuate forthwith' was given and children labelled like suitcases and befriended by an army of teachers were sent from the arms of crying mothers to a new and strange life in the country.

Operation Pied Piper started officially on September 1st 1939 and 3.5 million children were relocated. It was accepted that if you had a spare room you were to give a child a home. The government had spent a year surveying available housing but certain quotas were overestimated and details were incorrect, so many children arrived in the wrong area or were sent to an address where there was not enough room. Some evacuees will forever have memories of being lined up in a cold village hall, clutching a gas mask and a food parcel and waiting to be picked.

The cultural impact of moving children used to an urban environment to a rural landscape would be disorientating at the best of times, but the additional trauma of separation from families and isolation made the lives of many quite difficult. The evacuation spawned a plethora of children's fiction, in particular *The Lion, the Witch and the Wardrobe*. In this novel C.S. Lewis creates a fantastical journey for the children who have been evacuated to a large country house as they daringly step into the wardrobe, through the fur coats and out into the land of Narnia.

The children came from the East End of London and were from the same family. The eldest evacuee was twelve-year-old Bob who along with his brothers John and Freddie, and a sister, were all evacuated to Somerset in 1940. Their mother had kept Freddie, the youngest, at home initially but sent him back to Somerset when the Blitz started. Harold's brother had a girl staying with his family who knew Bob, as they had sat next to each other at school and their mothers had worked

Harold and Doris (both in their eighties) sitting on the commemorative bench.

Retirement photo – Harold had been with Marshalsea Hydraulics for 33 years. The presentation was made by John Bennett, Chairman and Tony Logan, Managing Director, and Harold received a carriage clock.

together in Silvertown. Bob eventually married this fellow evacuee and they have lived in Bridgwater ever since. Doris and Harold never had children so they appreciated the time they had with their evacuees, becoming very close to Bob who would always be like a son to them.

THE LONDON BLITZ

When the Second World War was declared it was thought likely that British cities, and in particular London, would be the target of air raids. It was to take a year before more than 1,000 Luftwaffe planes, under the orders of Hermann Goering, crossed the channel with London in their sights. The first wave of the Blitz began over London on September 7th 1940 and focused on the Port of London, which lies along the banks of the River Thames, and the industrial area (mainly the East End). When the Luftwaffe bombed Buckingham Palace the Queen Mother famously said 'she would now be able to look the East End in the face'. This bombardment carried on for 57 days. Initially the city's defences were wholly inadequate to day and night attacks but by September 11th anti-aircraft attacks were helping to boost civilian morale.

It was a David and Goliath situation, and the Germans destroyed large swathes of this beautiful city. Fire consumed large areas and people took shelter wherever they could, especially in the underground stations. The sirens that rang out over London were followed by the terrifying noise of the guns, or batches of dazzling white ferocious incendiary bombs, lighting the way for the next swarm of bombers. The image of St Paul's Cathedral surrounded by fire with its gigantic dome piercing a red sky, will stay in many memories forever. The sheer strength and determination of Londoners in the face of this onslaught is legendary and the courage shown by many who carried on with their daily lives is remarkable.

After the war Harold worked long days and had little time for leisure or a hobby although both he and Doris thoroughly enjoyed gardening. Harold also loved to play skittles and was in the industrial league, playing at many local working men's clubs. Doris helped her sister run a pub in Creech St Michael, much to Harold's displeasure. He had never liked pubs and would say that if he was dying of thirst he would rather walk past fifty pubs. When her sister decided to give up the lease the brewery wanted Harold and Doris to take over, but Harold declined the offer.

As the 1950s approached Britain settled into an austere lull. Harold was still working at Marshalsea and one afternoon there was a knock on his office door. Herbert Froneck was the chief designer at Marshalsea and had been with the company since the war. He had been parachuted into Britain for the purpose of espionage, but had been captured and became a prisoner of war. Although Harold despised him for what he stood for, he strongly admired him for his creativity and intelligence. Froneck knew that Harold was going to be offered an elevated managerial position and advised him that under no circumstances should he turn any offer down. Sure enough, Mr Bennett came down from London on a Monday afternoon and stayed at the County Hotel in Taunton until Wednesday afternoon. He made Harold an offer which he accepted, and he worked in this position until his retirement on March 30th 1976.

Harold always rode to work on a motorbike and was an avid motorbike enthusiast throughout his life, but realised one day that he really should learn to drive a car. As the company was associated with the motor industry, they employed driving instructors, so he asked for tuition. He already had a license for all groups of driving and didn't need an L-plate. During one of the lessons the instructor seemed to be writing in a book and Harold asked him if everything was all right, to which he replied, "Harold! I'd drive to London with you!" The first car that Harold bought was a Vauxhall Corsa which he drove until he was ninety, eventually passing it on to Bob Jones' grandson Miles when he was learning to drive.

For many years Harold and Doris enjoyed the Lanes living next door and they were more like best friends than neighbours. Things changed though when Ron was offered a job in Taunton and as it was too far to travel, they decided to move. Life in Outwood would never be the same. Soon afterwards Doris saw an aunt whose husband sold his farm in Ogsall and bought a cottage in Thurloxton, which was now lying empty. When Harold and Doris were offered the opportunity of moving they jumped at the chance. Bob Jones was on hand to help them move and as this was Doris' last remaining relative they inherited the cottage when her aunt died. The stipulation was that it was theirs as long as they lived, but when they passed away it was to be left to the National Animal Welfare Trust.

Harold and Doris never ventured abroad but they did enjoy spending time by the sea in North Devon. In return for helping the landlady of their local pub, the Green Dragon, Doris was given unlimited use of a caravan at the Lagoon View Caravan Park in Instow. When Harold finished work on Fridays he would return home to Doris, who would have the picnic basket ready, and off they would go. The pretty village of Instow with its Regency style terraces looks over the estuary where the River Taw and the River Torridge meet. It is situated between Bideford and Barnstaple so Harold and Doris would visit these towns often. After a day's driving, Harold and Doris liked to have a proper Devonshire cream tea at the Commodore Hotel before returning to the caravan and listening to the waves as they fell into a blissful slumber. Sometimes they took a stroll along Marine Parade to the sand dunes at the end, eating rock salmon and chips out of newspaper, or walked along the Tarka Trail, which is named after the route that Tarka the Otter took.

Harold's 80th birthday cake complete with iced cabbages.

Harold and Doris with the evacuees as adults.

When Harold and Doris reached an age where living alone was proving to be difficult thoughts turned to a sheltered housing scheme, or a place for both of them in a residential care home. Friends rallied round and discovered a comfortable double room at Sydenham House in Bridgwater which both Harold and Doris liked. They were just settling into a new routine when Doris was taken ill and went to a nursing home for treatment. During this uncertain time Harold was very distressed, as he felt in his heart that she wasn't coming back, and greatly appreciated his evacuee friend Bob Jones being there for support and comfort. Doris recently passed away and Harold is doing his best to come to terms with life without her. He feels like it is getting better and was very pleased that he saw her one more time. What he misses most is that he will never hear her voice again.

Doris was buried at Thurloxton and when Harold's turn comes he will be cremated and his ashes will be sprinkled over her grave. They were married for seventy years and he will never forget her. Harold remembers a wonderful woman who was forever in the kitchen baking cakes for everyone and often just gave them away to the birds.

Harold thinks that Sydenham House is a wonderful place and the staff are kind and friendly. He especially likes it when the entertainer comes to the home. He puts on a record and Harold is off, singing along to all the classics. Harold is so enthusiastic that the entertainer comes over with his microphone and holds it out for him to sing into. Harold's smile is broad and happy when he tells his story.

MINNIE TAYLOR

'I always had hobbies – I didn't like to be idle'

MINNIE WAS BORN on 30th December 1909 in Washford, a small village in the Old Cleeve parish in South-West Somerset. It is probably best known for Cleeve Abbey, a medieval Cisterian monastery, which has one of the finest remaining English cloisters. Minnie is the last remaining of one sister and four brothers who all grew up to have diverse careers: one became a grocer; one a schoolteacher; one a member of the Royal Air Force; and the youngest brother worked for the Telephone and Cable Company laying cables, even travelling to Paris.

Minnie's mother Kate Peglar was from Gloucestershire and she was a children's nurse for a well-respected shipping family in Bristol. Sometimes she accompanied the family for a day out and they often enjoyed walking through Weacombe, a steep wooded valley that runs down from the Quantock Hills. Minnie's father was a builder who was doing some restoration work at a big house which was nestled in the valley. He plucked up the courage to talk to Kate and they began a courtship that became a long and happy marriage.

Washford was a pleasant place for a child to grow up. Before Minnie started school the family moved from McKinley Terrace where she was born to live with her grandparents. Her grandmother was losing her sight because of cataracts but insufficient medical help was available, and they both needed the support of their family. Her grandparents' house had a big garden with pear trees, and the Washford stream ran along the bottom. The old Mineral Line was nearby and although trains very rarely used the line, Minnie can remember the occasional train going from Watchet to Roadwater when she was young.

D.O.B. 30/12/1909

THE OLD MINERAL LINE

This was an independent railway line covering 11 miles that connected the old harbour town of Watchet with the now long-abandoned ironstone mines and villages high up on the Brendon Hills. The line now has a certain place in local folklore, and original buildings and landmarks can be traced along the route. The railway was built between 1857 and 1864 to convey iron ore from the Brendon Hills and on to the port of Watchet, where it was transported from ships over to South Wales. The iron ore deposits were rich in minerals and even though they were highly fragmented they were low in sulphur and phosphorous, which proved to be an advantage when iron-making technology became more advanced.

Right: Minnie at school with the Norman sisters (Ruby, Hazel, Trixie) and Eileen Edwards, 1920.

Far right: Taken at the rectory at Old Cleeve. The rector's daughter held Girls Friendly Society meetings and this is a picture of Minnie aged 13 dancing with friends Clarice Bennett, Maude Webber, Lily Lewis, Winnie Howe and her cousin Mattie Taylor, 1922.

Minnie playing cricket in the field outside Claydon Close, 1929.

At one point on the route there is a breathtaking drop of 1,200 feet into the hamlet of Comberrow, one of the most remote wooded enclaves in the West Country. From here the railway and wagons had to travel slowly down the steep slope or were hoisted up the incline. The railway was also opened for passenger travel between Watchet and Comberrow in 1865 and if passengers wished to travel beyond to Gupworthy they could travel free of charge on open wagons with bench seats.

The railway had provided work and short-lived prosperity in this remote landscape, where agriculture was the main source of employment. The workers from these villages were joined by engineers from around the country and miners from Cornwall, and at the junction of the B3224 and B3190 stands a Methodist chapel which was used for the spiritual needs of the miners and their families.

By 1877 the mines had reached a peak of 47,000 tonnes and these small communities worked together. But thereafter steel prices plummeted, and mining ceased in 1883. However the line was still used to provide a limited passenger service until 1898. During the Second World War the rails were commandeered for scrap and the old Mineral Line officially closed in 1924. It is now enjoyed as a pleasant walk, and at Comberrow the station master's house is occupied, with part of the platform still visible. It now provides a trip back in time, following the grassy bed of the line as it passes through sleepy hamlets reminiscent of another era.

On Saturday mornings the children had certain jobs to do before they could go out to play. Minnie's favourite game was marbles and she kept her treasured ones in a small cloth bag: the turtle with its waxy streaks of green and yellow; the red Devil's eye; and the Lutz with its silver swirl which she won from her friend Betty with a clever thumb flick. The lane behind her house was quiet and sometimes they would play marbles on the main road, which very rarely saw anything travelling along it. One afternoon they were shocked to see a policeman coming along on a horse and trap and ran up a country lane to hide. The children weren't supposed to play on the main road but Minnie felt a fool, as they had left chalk patterns from the game of marbles all over the road.

Minnie went to a Church of England school in the village. Although she wasn't terribly keen on school she quite liked Geography and looked forward to Tuesdays, when the children walked to the Railway Inn for cookery classes in the old club rooms behind the pub. Concerts were often held in the main assembly room, and there was great excitement when it was Empire Day. The girls were allowed to go to school with their hair curled and done up with rags and ribbons, and they sang 'Jerusalem' and danced around the Maypole. As all the men were away during the war, Washford School had a female headmistress called Miss Palmer who was very strict and quite frightening. Minnie has little memory of the First World War but she can remember her father coming home one day with a big wooden horse for her younger brother that had been made by a German prisoner of war.

EMPIRE DAY

A national day of remembrance, Empire Day was first celebrated in Britain on May 24th 1902 (Queen Victoria's birthday) and was recognised as an annual event in 1916. It was seen as the opportunity to encourage patriotic feeling and raise awareness of the British Empire and all its achievements and strengths. The Empire Movement was founded by Lord Meath and his watch words were: 'responsibility, sympathy, duty and self-sacrifice'.

All schoolchildren celebrated by singing patriotic songs such as 'Jerusalem' and 'God Save The Queen' and by pinning a small metal badge with a tiny Union Jack to their lapel. There were inspirational speeches and stories of heroic adventure which were followed by Maypole dancing, concerts and parties. All children especially looked forward to Empire Day as they were given the afternoon off and went home to fireworks and gaiety.

By the 1950s the Empire was in decline as Britain's relationship with other countries was changing as they began to celebrate their own identities. Empire Day was renamed Commonwealth Day in 1958, partly due to political correctness and the politics of the far left who had begun to attack British Imperialism. The multicultural nature of cities today owes much to the notion of Empire, as part of the reason people migrated to British shores was the economic conditions created by Empire.

When Minnie left school people had to take any job that was offered. She was quite keen to do dressmaking, so she did a three-year apprenticeship with Mrs Maunder, who lived in a big private house on Holloway Street in Minehead. Although it was tiring work and she only earned three shillings a week, she had enormous fun and was grateful that she was doing a job she wanted to do. She took the train into town every day, which she liked as it passed through Blue Anchor, a seaside resort she often visited with friends. When she finished work she would wander down to the seafront, and if it was a nice day she might take a deckchair to the edge of the sands and buy a lemon ice. If there was a chill wind she went to the Mermaid Tearooms, although her friends teased her about the tale of Mother Leakey, the whistling ghost who whistled up a storm whenever her son's ship neared port.

Minnie bumped into a friend one afternoon who asked if she was going to the dance at the

Portrait 1930s – she bought the dress but spilt something on the bottom half, which is why only the top half is shown.

Minnie with her sister Kathleen, niece Daphne and Cecil, 1930s.

Minnie at Blue Anchor, 1931.

Minnie and Cecil on their wedding day, August 12th 1939, with her niece Daphne and Henry Tame, the lodger.

Right: Wedding day in Old Cleeve with their parents. Minnie is wearing the dress and posy she made.

Far right: Minnie in Cornwall with Cecil, 1950s.

village hall in Old Cleeve. These dances were an opportunity for local bands to play to an audience, and Minnie and her friends would look forward to the weekend with relish. Although she liked to follow all the latest fashions she was often too lazy to make them as she spent all her time making dresses, so Minnie and her friends bought second-hand clothes from a lady who ran a little shop at Torre. She had just bought a lovely dance dress made of blue georgette with a lace frill at the bottom and was glad of an occasion to wear it.

Minnie had told her friend she was going to the dance and was informed that a nice young man called Cecil Taylor would be there. She was curious as she had met him before at a dance but he hadn't asked to walk her home which she thought was strange, as he hadn't taken his eyes off her all night. As she entered the hall she noticed the tall dark young man looking over and looked down, brushing something from her dress. She had a feeling she might have company for this evening's moonlit walk.

Minnie and Cecil were married on August 12th 1939 at St Andrew's church in Old Cleeve on the hottest day of the year. She wore a blue satin dress and carried a posy of hydrangeas, both of which she had made herself. The whole family attended and her father gave Minnie away. Her niece Daphne was a bridesmaid. She is now in her seventies and still visits Minnie. After the ceremony everyone went back to the house in Washford to celebrate, and the next day Minnie and Cecil took the train to Bridgwater to stay with her sister for a few days. This was the calm before the storm, as the war broke out a matter of weeks later.

When they returned from their trip Minnie and Cecil moved in with his parents who lived just off the High Street in Carhampton. It was a large house with 4 or 5 bedrooms and Minnie and Cecil had their own section with a passageway that joined the main house. Henry and Bertha Taylor were quite comfortable and had made sure their son wanted for nothing. Henry had a small business selling the finest bone china and he acquired stock from bankrupt factories in Birmingham. He kept the stock in one of the rooms of the house and travelled around the area selling the china from his horse and cart.

The time Minnie and Cecil spent with his parents was a happy time and apart from sharing a staircase they had total privacy. Minnie got on well with both Henry and Bertha, although at times she found Bertha quite old fashioned. Behind the utility shed there was a large garden that led on to an abundant orchard and the neighbouring farmer let Minnie keep chickens on a small corner of his land. During the war if you hadn't any children you had to work, and Minnie had

a job in a local grocer's shop. Cecil was a gardener by trade, working for private homes, and as he was a horticultural worker he didn't have to enlist as he was playing an active part in food production for the country. Most of the time the war seemed a million miles away but Minnie remembers planes in the sky, and the sound of bombers overhead will always be a lasting memory. A bomb was dropped near Old Cleeve and the Germans also dropped a bomb one bright moonlit night which made a crater in the ground in a field near Carhampton. It seemed that it was a tomato farm with row upon row of greenhouses, and the reflection of the moon on glass was seen as a target.

Minnie and Cecil never moved out of the house in Carhampton, as his parents passed away within a short time of each other and he inherited the house. Minnie continued to work in the grocer's shop in Washford and she would travel there on the local bus. Although they never had a car, Cecil had a motorbike that he rode to work at the Parade Nurseries behind the Almshouses in Minehead. This row of cottages tucked away behind the Parade was built in 1630 by a local merchant mariner, Robert Quirke, and was incredibly lucky to survive a ferocious fire in the summer of 1791. The fire broke out in the mill at the bottom of Bampton Street, destroying most of Minehead's Lower Town. If Minnie and Cecil ever ventured further afield it was either to go to Taunton, which was a treat, or on holiday to the Midlands where her brothers lived, or to visit Derbyshire and the Peak District.

Minnie with her mother, brother, sister in law and eldest brother, 1950s.

99th birthday – Christmas time!

Cecil worked until he was seventy and after only a few years of retirement Minnie noticed that his memory was failing. This was to be the start of Cecil's health deteriorating and proved to be a very difficult time for Minnie. Cecil died at home and Minnie's relatives supported her throughout this painful time. Being part of a loving united family made things easier. The days stretched ahead of her at first and she felt lonely and sad. The large house in Carhampton seemed to be a burden and once she was on her own she realised she didn't need such a big house. She admits to herself now that she had never really liked the place, and after six months she sold it and bought a bungalow in Castlemead in Washford.

The decision to move to Washford was a revelation for Minnie. She adored her little bungalow and before long she was filling her time with numerous hobbies, as she has never liked to be idle. She became a member of the Washford Goodwill Club which gave her the opportunity to make new friends, and she would often help organise social evenings. The club met every Thursday afternoon in the old reading rooms in Washford and held whist drives, bingo and dressmaking circles. Minnie had always enjoyed her own company and started to knit different costumes for dolls and cuddly toys. She has a varied collection and has been inspired by fashions of all kind.

Minnie lived in her bungalow until between 10 and 12 years ago, when she moved to Peerage Court in Minehead. The small flat that this sheltered housing block has provided is more than adequate for Minnie. When she first came to Peerage Court she would go into Minehead and wander along the Parks Walk to Bratton Ball or have tea in the Bandstand Café in Blenheim Gardens. There were also activities organised in the communal rooms in Peerage Court that she joined in with but now she doesn't tend to go out very much and prefers to stay in her room. She has been very happy here and is surrounded by all the trinkets and mementos that she has gathered throughout her life, including her incredible collection of owls. Even though Minnie may not remember every single detail of her life, she remembers what is important and treasures these memories.

WINNIE WESTON

'We didn't do anything extraordinary.
I took no notice because that was my life. We were happy'.

WINNIE WAS BORN in Bridgwater on December 9th 1908 and had an older brother, Stanley, and a younger brother, Bill. Winnie's father was a shirt cutter and worked at Pearsall's at the top of East Reach in Taunton. Her mother had a delicate constitution and died when Winnie was quite young so she left school at 12 to look after the family.

Before her mother died Winnie was taught to have a routine. The tiny back kitchen was cold in winter which helped, as having no fridge meant that you had to keep the milk bottles in a metal bucket to keep cool. Some households had a well in the back garden which you could lower your bucket down into. One of the first jobs of the day was to collect water from the barrel in the garden and put the pots on to boil. She built the fires for the day using bunches of faggots which were kept for winter fuel in the shed. Then Winnie made the beds and set about doing the washing. She put the clothes in an old furnace, lit the fire underneath and boiled them. Sometimes she cut a chunk of soap from a big bar but if the clothes were really stained she grated the soap and left the clothes to soak. When everything was clean she put it through the mangle and then hung it out to dry in the blustery day. Sometimes in winter the clothes froze on the line.

Winnie had always enjoyed cooking and had watched her mother avidly as she creamed the butter and sugar together when she was making sweet fruit pies. When her father came home with a bucket of elvers she poured boiling water over them and then rinsed them, leaving them overnight in salt water. They were lovely fried in foaming butter for breakfast. Sometimes her father brought home a side of ham which would hang on a big hook by the fire to smoke. There was always a pot of stock or broth on the stove, regularly topped up with bones from the butcher and the odd carrot or onion. She did her best to look after the men, darning their socks and making her father hot whisky toddys if he had a chill.

When she had some spare time Winnie liked to socialise with a group of friends. Sometimes they all cycled down to the river or went dancing together. She arrived at Margot's house one evening and there was a new face in the room and she was introduced to a young man from Bristol. Arthur was from Fishponds and he was a delivery driver for the large fruit and vegetable market in the centre of town. She remembers him removing his cap and holding out his hand. Her hand stayed in his for what seemed like forever and then "we were stuck together, inseparable". The others were almost jealous that Winnie and Arthur got on so well together. They were married in All Saints' church, Trull in 1933.

D.O.B. 09/12/1908

All Saints' church, Trull.

The only job that Winnie ever had was working as a dinner lady at Priory School, which she did until after the war. The children arrived on an old Bedford coach that stank of petrol and the fare was an old penny coin. It was a very hard job and all the dinner ladies wore big white wraparound coats and sturdy black shoes. Winnie worked from 9 until 4 during the week and on Saturday mornings she went in to clean the ovens. The kitchen equipment was basic, functional and scrubbed. The store rooms at the far end of the kitchen were stacked floor to ceiling with huge tins of ingredients and sacks of salt, flour and Bournville cocoa. Winnie cooked large amounts of food in huge aluminium canisters. There were huge hunks of boiled beef surrounded by soft carrots or mince and onions and the children had semolina for pudding with a dollop of raspberry jam. On Friday it would be a treat to have fried fish or spam fritters. She worked with a girl called May West who was short and dark and the headmistress Miss Wilson always walked with little clipped steps, leaving a flourish of skirt behind.

SCHOOL DINNERS

The whole ethos for school dinners is that they hold a vital place in the national policy for the nutrition and well-being of children. The first time school dinners were provided was as an act of charity in the nineteenth century. In 1906 when the liberal government was elected, reforms were introduced which improved the provision of school meals in response to the poor health of many children in Britain. In 1944 school meals were made compulsory. Meals would be provided at the basic cost of the ingredients while the staff and kitchen were paid for by the authorities. The diet ensured low quantities of fat and sugar. Throughout the 1950s-70s the school kitchens continued to produce steaming quantities of stews, boiled cabbage, and great vats of tapioca pudding, and where would school dinners have been without the humble prune? In 1980 Margaret Thatcher passed an Education Act that first eliminated school milk and then in order to regulate school dinners she introduced Compulsory Competitive Tendering. In 2005 school dinners became an election issue thanks to celebrity chef Jamie Oliver.

During the war Arthur spent six years in the Royal Air Force and was stationed in the Middle East and India. He was demobbed in 1947 and Winnie was relieved when he finally came home as she thought he was never coming back, and his son Derek had missed him dreadfully. When Arthur was away Winnie was at home with Derek and Grandad Durston who had come to live with them. The family were now living in a terraced house in Taunton and when Derek was old enough Winnie would send him to see Mr Bowyer on Queen Street to pay the rent where the amount and date were noted in a little blue book.

Taunton had its fair share of dangers during the war. One day when Derek was at junior school, two incendiary bombs fell on Eastleigh Road and two semi-detached houses took a direct hit. Derek and a friend cycled out from school to have a look. There were two more bombs out near Silk Mills and the boys went looking for shrapnel. It was quite likely to have been caused by a German bomber on its way home from bombing Bristol which had released the last shell rather than take it home to Germany.

In the years after the war communities pulled together in an effort to strengthen the country and old friendships grew stronger. Winnie had first met her best friend Nelly Moggridge at school when the main building was within the churchyard. It was always a little spooky when walking home on a November evening alone. They had continued to grow closer over the years and had been part of the same group of friends when Winnie first met Arthur. It seemed like she and Nelly had been together forever and Winnie was treated like one of the family. Nelly's father Percy had been left 12 terraced houses in Trull by his grandfather and most of his family lived in them. He was very good friends with Arthur and tried to persuade him to buy one of the houses at an incredible discount of £475, but Arthur didn't have the money and was too proud to borrow. Before Arthur returned from the war Winnie lived with Nelly in Trull for 2 years, while Derek stayed with his Auntie Mandy and Uncle Fred in Rowbarton. They were not actually relations but just very close friends. Over the years the Moggridges and the Westons spent a lot of time together.

There were younger brothers and cousins who got on well with Derek which made him happy, as being an only child made parts of his childhood quite lonely. The Moggridges were quite well off so every Christmas Winnie and her family went to Trull for a combined celebration that sometimes lasted for days. Everyone got caught up in this social whirl. Winnie didn't care for alcohol but Arthur enjoyed a light ale. The men mainly drank cider and the women giggled about the new dresses from America, and games such as pass the parcel or charades would be played. Everyone went to the Winchester Arms while the turkey was roasting and on the way home the young lads would be slightly giddy with ale and threaten the girls with the village stocks.

As the years passed by the main purpose of Winnie's life was her family. The important things were making sure that her men had a clean shirt, the sandwiches were made and packed the night before, and that the house was tidy. Winnie had always been a little over protective of her son from as far back as when he was a small boy coming home with grazed knees. When he was a teenager working at Whites on Saturdays she wouldn't let him have a motorbike and would say, "over my dead body". Derek had coveted this immaculate piece of machinery, an amazing speedway bike that belonged to Cyril Quick whose father worked with Arthur. He never got to ride it. When he was 21 Derek left home to join the RAF to do his National Service. When Winnie had to say goodbye she cried for days. It was the mid 1950s and there was trouble in the Middle East due to the Suez crisis. There were serious fuel shortages as no one could use the canal and petrol prices went sky high. It seemed that Winnie's prayers may have been answered as Derek was shipped straight out to Malta, avoiding the very real dangers in Egypt.

THE SUEZ CRISIS

This war was fought by Britain, France and Israel against Egypt and began on 29th October 1956. It followed Egypt's decision to nationalise the Suez Canal after Britain and the US withdrew an offer to fund the construction of the Aswan Dam, situated across the River Nile.

The Suez Canal was opened in 1869 and was the only 'bridge' between Africa and Asia. The shortest ocean link between the Mediterranean Ocean and the Indian Ocean, it helped ease commerce for trading nations. It was of vital importance and a strategic intersection. During WWI Britain and France closed it to non-allied shipping and after WWII it became a passage for the shipment of oil. By 1955, two thirds of Europe's oil was passing through the Suez Canal.

Trouble was brewing when King Farouk and the Egyptian monarchy was removed in a

Calway House.

Winnie and friend at
Calway House.

military coup led by Gamal Abdul Nasser, who established an Eqyptian republic. For Nasser this heralded a new period of modernisation and social reform. Britain did its best to mend Anglo-Egyptian relations, even offering to terminate British rule in Sudan and an evacuation of British troops from the Suez Base, but Nasser was not prepared to co-operate. He believed that neither his regime nor Egypt's independence would be safe until Egypt established itself as head of the Arab world. Nasser's response was a series of challenges to British influence in the region that would culminate in the Suez Crisis.

After President Eisenhower withdrew all American financial aid and the canal was nationalised Britain's main interests in the area were badly damaged, so military intervention was ordered to avoid the complete collapse of British prestige in the region. To avoid angering their allies in Washington, the British government signed a secret military pact with France and Israel that was aimed at regaining control of Suez.

On October 29th 1956 Israel launched an attack on Egypt and seized control of the Mitla Pass. As an act of intervention Britain and France seized the canal but given an ultimatum, Nasser refused. What followed was to cause widespread outrage as British and French troops invaded Port Said, taking control of the Suez Canal. The US, USSR and UN all condemned this military action and Anglo-American relations were decidedly frosty for some while.

Winnie and Arthur were able to spend quality time together and they enjoyed going to the cinema on Saturday afternoons. It is quite likely that one of the films they may have seen was Cecil B. DeMille's *Samson and Delilah* which depicted the popular biblical story, starring Victor Mature and the bewitching Hedy Lamarr. They may also have seen MGM's expensive romantic adventure *King Solomon's Mines* which was filmed on location in Africa. Both of these films were designed to lure people back into the cinema as by the mid 1950s more than half of Hollywood's productions were being made in colour to get people's attention away from the novelty of the black and white television set.

Whilst Arthur was at work one day he had a small stroke. This affected his memory and at times he was uncertain who Winnie was. He did make a recovery but had to give up his old job as the heavy lifting was too much. As he was never an idle man he became an odd job man for a local firm. Four days before Christmas 1962 Arthur died aged 58. Derek and his wife Ann moved into the house with Winnie and they continued to live with her for company and support. They would live together for the next thirty five years.

As Derek and Ann lived exceptionally busy lives and were out at work all day Winnie resumed an earlier role as home keeper and helped around the house, went shopping and cooked all the meals. She lived a quiet life and most of her enjoyment was gained from watching television especially soap operas, a good film or a classical musical. On Saturday afternoons Derek dropped his mother off in Taunton to have a wander around the shops, picking her up a couple of hours later. As the decades changed, society did too and Winnie noticed a change in the town and decided not to go anymore.

CORONATION STREET

This wonderful nostalgic view of working class life is the longest running and most watched British drama series of its kind. It features the most famous row of terraced houses and a local pub on the corner, the 'Rovers', which is the main meeting place for the show's characters.

Coronation Street is a prime time soap opera set in Weatherfield, a fictional area of Salford. It was created by Tony Warren in 1959, who turned to his colleague late one night and said ...

"Olive, I've got this wonderful idea for a television series. I can see a little back street in Salford with a pub at one end and a shop at the other and I can see all the lives of the people there, just ordinary things ..."

It was first broadcast on December 6th 1960 and although the success of the show was initially doubted by the television company, viewers were drawn to the show, won over by the earthiness of its 'ordinary' characters and their broad Northern dialect. The show's famous theme music, a cornet piece accompanied by a brass band is reminiscent of Northern band music. The theme tune has now been updated and accompanies a new credit sequence featuring images of Manchester and Weatherfield.

Over the years there have been many fascinating characters and brilliantly written scripts for the actors to work with. The Greek Chorus of Ena Sharples, Minnie Caldwell and Martha Longhurst, sitting in the snug and passing judgement on one and all; Elsie Tanner and Bet Lynch who were both icons of a generation, Lynch mirroring the vulnerability and strength of her predecessor. The acid tongue but razor sharp wit of matriarchs like Blanche Hunt and the familiarity and endearing bickering of the 'Street's' famous double acts like Jack and Vera Duckworth and Stan and Hilda Ogden, complete with flying plaster ducks on the wall. It's all about the light touches. Storylines continue to address social issues and in this portrayal of the urban working classes, with its laughter and tears, the ordinary lives of others are brilliantly drawn.

Winnie and other residents at the opening of Calway House by HRH The Duchess of Gloucester, May 2007.

Winnie at Calway House.

Winnie started visiting Calway House as a day care resident and gradually started to spend more time there, eventually moving into the home permanently in 1992. The home is surrounded by gardens and is in a quiet residential part of Taunton. She has seen the home change greatly as it has been at the centre of many renovation projects and has now been rebuilt as a larger modern complex. She thinks it is a lovely place with a homely atmosphere and that the people are really friendly. There are a dedicated team who entertain, support and care for Winnie and all the residents. Derek admits that as she lived with him for so long it took a while to sink in but she seems happier now and they visit often. Her life is now very much in the past and she shares her thoughts with me by telling me ... "I don't mind being on my own. I often sit here when I'm on my own and think about what we used to do, what we used to say, where we used to go. Life was always a struggle but we got by".

HILDA GOULDING

'I am old now but I have had a good life that has seen all the changes most will not see in a lifetime, some good and some bad.'

'I AM OLD NOW but I have had a good life that has seen all the changes most will not see in a lifetime, some good and some bad. But the truth of it is, for all our wars and peace and fears, I know I could have sat on that broken stile looking over at the Tor until the cows came home to milk and I would have waited for that fair haired boy in breeches and braces, a bunch of Sweet Williams bunched in his hand, until I'd seen the end of my days and I'd lay my head for a sleep and remember.'

Hilda was born in Street on April 5th 1906 and has lived there all her life. Hilda was one of 12 children and lost a five year old brother when she was very young. She is very proud to say they never quarrelled even though they all shared the attic rooms, and often the sound of iron springs would keep her awake at night as the younger children squirmed around in their tiny beds. Hilda was a blessing to her mother Georgina May Webber as girls were a helpful commodity amongst a male dominated family. Hilda's father was a shoemaker who had worked in Glasgow for many years before settling in Street, where there was plenty of work due to the Clarks Shoe Factory. Her grandparents lived on the other side of the street and her grandfather would tell stories of when he was a young man and served as a Royal Marine.

D.O.B. 05/04/1909

THE ROYAL MARINES

Proud to have Her Majesty Queen Elizabeth II as its Commander in Chief, the Royal Marines combined with the Royal Navy and the Royal Fleet Auxiliary form the Naval Service. They officially formed part of the service in 1755 but the first time English soldiers went to sea was to fight the Dutch on October 28th 1664, under the title of the Duke Of Albany Maritime Regiment of Foot. They were part of the mobilisation for the second Anglo Dutch War with Britain trying to end the Dutch domination of world trade. Fighting began in earnest with the Battle of Lowestoft and although they achieved a victory there would be many defeats to come.

Throughout the eighteenth and nineteenth centuries the Royal Marines played a major part in the fight to win the British the largest empire ever created. They arrived on Australian shores in 1788; were part of the bombardment of Algiers in 1816 and, a little closer to home, helped maintain civil order in Newcastle and Northern Ireland during the coal dispute of 1831. When

Clarks Shoe Factory.

World War I started Britain had the largest fleet in commission in the world and in 1945 the Royal Marines took on the responsibility for the training of the British Commandos. The achievements of the Royal Marines have been prodigious and they continue to meet the nation's needs whenever necessary.

Georgina worked for Clarks stitching shoes so the children took it in turns to help with the housework. They swept and mopped the white tiled floors, getting water from the stand pipe at the end of the street or from the barrel in the garden where the rain water had collected. Hilda helped do the washing by hand using a dolly and a mangle and dried clothes next to the open fire. The clothes would then be pressed with a big flat stone iron. There was a coal range in the kitchen although some of the cooking was done over the fire, grabbing a pot from one of the iron hooks. There was also a bread oven and often one of the children would be sent into town for a couple of pennyworth of yeast which would steep in warm water by the fire. There was no fridge and all the food was kept in the pantry where there was a big marble slab, perfect for rolling out pastry for pies. The milk jug sat with a cloth draped over it. With everyone mucking in, there was no hierarchy and everyone was treated the same.

When Hilda was approaching her teens the family moved to Grange Avenue to a house called The Laurels, where her parents would live for many years. Hilda went to a boarding school until she was 13 and then carried on at a continuation school for two days a week as she had found work at Clarks Shoe Factory, stitching labels. On Sunday mornings she went to Sunday school from early morning until teatime where they would read the scriptures and be given stamps that were all about certain sections of the bible. Church was to become a main social engagement and on a Sunday morning Hilda would leave early to take Holy Communion before heading home to put the brisket in the oven and peel the vegetables. Some Sundays, if the weather was good, they would take the steam train to Burnham for a day out. Hilda was popular in many circles and would become a member of the choir, making many friends.

It was whilst working at Clarks Shoe Factory that she first met Ronald Goulding. She had noticed this tall blond chap working on the leathers and had enquired shyly from her friends as to who he was. Apart from the occasional stolen glance she could not pluck up the courage to talk to him until just before Christmas when they bumped into each other at the Christmas Fatstock Show in Glastonbury. This was a special livestock market with collared cows in large pens and sheep and pigs in the smaller cages. There were many local butchers competing against each other, especially on the open evening when all the meat would be on display.

There was a large crowd at Parsons Field that day and some of her friends had draped pink bunting between the trees, tied in big bows around the thick trunks. The butchers had been in friendly but tough competition with each other since early spring, feeding their livestock well and whispering encouragement when noone was around. The hard work had paid off as much attention was focused on a fine display of tightly packed ribs of beef and shoulders of pork, bunches of thyme tucked in the folds and marbled with creamy fat. The pride of the show though was the frenetic noise and bustle of the turkeys in the large canvas tent in the centre of the field. It was three weeks until Christmas.

Hilda remembers that in amongst all that commotion she saw Ronald with his fair hair and soft ruddy cheeks that dimpled when he smiled. When she saw him, she just knew and when they danced together later after the annual supper she felt like she was lost in a meadow. They saw each other constantly. He lived with his mother in Glastonbury in a small grey slate cottage covered in wisteria with a crooked weathervane perched on the roof. The sound of hammer striking metal would ring out from the forge next door as they sat under a tree in the garden, hands clasped. He would walk from Manor House Road in Glastonbury all the way to where Hilda lived at the Laurels in Street, and he would come and see her every night. She definitely felt that he was her soul mate.

Hilda.

GLASTONBURY TOR

It is known as one of the Celtic 'perpetual choirs' and is said to maintain the spiritual integrity of Britain. The air, cool water and essence of this magical place is quite unique. Glastonbury Tor is found as part of the landscape of Avalon and can be seen from a distance, rising above the flat Summerland meadows of the Somerset Levels. In the mid 400s, at the time of St Patrick, there was a monks' retreat on the Tor and in 705 AD King Ine founded a monastery on this spot which became a Benedictine house in the tenth century. In the early 1100s the St Michael de Torre Chapel was built, but destroyed in an earthquake in 1275 which also devastated many houses and churches in the area. Rebuilt in the 1300s, the tower is all that remains.

Many myths and legends have been associated with Glastonbury Tor. There have always been stories that it is the home of Gwyn ap Nudd, Lord of the Underworld and King of the Fairies but the myth that really catches the imagination is that it is Avalon, the heart of Arthurian legend which is watched over by the powerful sorceress Morgan Le Fey. In 1190 AD two monks claimed to have discovered the graves of King Arthur and his queen Guinevere. Supposedly there was a coffin cut from a hollow log containing the bones of a 2.4 metre man with a damaged skull as well as smaller bones with wisps of yellow hair. The bones were then re-interred in a black marble tomb. Glastonbury continues to attract large crowds of visitors keen to feel its magical presence.

Glastonbury Tor.

Hilda and Ronald fell in love and on December 31st 1933 they were married at the parish church in Street. On the morning of the wedding Hilda felt so happy she could burst, hardly believing that this day had finally come. She can remember sitting on her bed with an eiderdown around her shoulders and watching a robin that had just landed on the window sill. It had snowed all night and the rooftops and paths were still unspoilt. Her mother came in with a tea tray and a plate of toasted muffins but she couldn't eat a thing as her stomach was full of tiny butterflies. Her dress was hanging on the back of the wardrobe and she thought it was the most beautiful thing she had ever seen. As she was now twenty-four she felt too old to wear white so she had chosen a lilac and royal blue silk dress and grey court shoes, although her proudest possession was a large blue picture hat which sat on the chest of drawers.

Hilda felt giddy in the church and when she had to say the words she could feel her legs shaking. Her Uncle Peter gave her away and his wife and Ronald's sister Gwen attended with

Hilda on holiday at
Burnham on Sea.

Clarks Shoe Factory.

Ron's retirement.

Sarah Flint, Hilda's music teacher playing the church organ. She remembers Ronald standing straight and proud beside her and when he kissed her she could taste a little rum on his lips.

Hilda and Ronald received many wedding presents from her work colleagues at the factory including a pink and white sifter from Mary in Accounts. Her mother gave them some hem-stitched sheets, her brother gave them a dinner service and her sister Rose gave them a china tea service. Then an old friend Jack Chislett drove them through banks of snow to catch the Great Western train from Highbridge, the tickets being an extra present from Ronald's father as he worked on the railways. They spent their honeymoon in a small hotel in Plymouth overlooking the sea and the Royal Marine barracks. The memory of her wedding day stands alone for Hilda as her happiest memory and her husband and her life with him were the only things that mattered to her.

When they returned from their honeymoon they went to work at Clarks and moved into a house that the company had provided. They carried on working there and were paid on a Friday, the money crisp and folded in a brown paper envelope. The payslip let them know what they had earned minus the money for rent. The firm thought it was good to deduct it first as it removed the temptation to spend it all on cider. Although it may seem like an affront to have some of your money taken, the employees understood the company's policy and how it was actually an act of kindness with no malice intended. It was always a true intention of the company to enrich and protect the community. Hilda's job at Clarks entailed the sewing and stitching of shoes and then she worked on the assembly floor, packing the shoes into large cardboard boxes before they were shipped around the country. She enjoyed the camaraderie and routine and never felt the need to look elsewhere for work. Many years later, Clarks would provide Hilda with a pension fund.

CLARKS

In 1825, James and Cyrus Clark were running a tannery in Street and the brothers looked around one afternoon at all the scraps of leather and animal hide and had a brainwave. The result of this epiphany was the very first Clarks shoe, the sheepskin slipper, uniquely made by hand. By 1842 Britain was riding the crest of a wave with Queen Victoria at the helm and sales of the 'Brown Petersburg' were averaging 1,000 pairs a month. The Clark brothers recruited many outworkers from the area to help meet the growing demand. They would collect the leather from the tannery, take it home and turn it in to slippers. This was often a family affair with everyone doing their share of cutting, stitching and sewing. Then afterwards the shoes would be exchanged for wages.

In 1863 Britain was hit by a recession and after taking advice from the Quaker community of which they were very much a part, it was decided that James's younger son William should take over. He was a visionary who completely modernised the manufacturing process, brought in the factory system and invested in the Singer sewing machine. He developed the business but kept true to his Quaker roots by investing in the community. He did this first and foremost by looking after his workers and built them all houses.

As the company enjoyed much success in the twentieth century, the first press advert appeared in 1936 and a chain of shops was launched called Peter Lord. During the war the main Clarks factory was used to make torpedoes and when there were shortages of leather, Clarks designed a unique wooden sole so supply could continue. The company continued to expand over the next few decades, helping Clarks to become one of the best known names in footwear.

Hilda and two friends around 1990.

Ronald didn't fight in the war but worked at Clarks all his life. During the war there were many evacuees in Street and it was generally accepted that if you had a spare room you were able to give a home to children from the towns and cities that were being bombed. As Hilda and Ronald were both working such long hours they were unable to have any children to stay. As they had not had any children of their own Hilda would have very much liked this, and she envied her friend Margaret who looked after a little girl from Plaistow.

The life that Hilda and Ronald enjoyed was quiet and simple. They both worked hard for Clarks and would stay there for all of their working lives. There was never any need to go further afield than Wells or Glastonbury as they had everything they needed on their doorstep. If they weren't working they would wander into town together and maybe stop for lunch somewhere. They liked to sit by the river and throw chunks of bread for the ducks and if it turned a little cold Ronald would drape his jacket around Hilda's shoulders. During the evenings Hilda and Ronald enjoyed staying at home and watching television or meeting friends in a local restaurant, where Hilda would enjoy a plate of steak and chips, a port and brandy and a good chat. Hilda had Ronald in her life for thirty five years before he died suddenly of a heart attack, and although she has lived alone for many years she still sees his face when she closes her eyes at night.

Left: Hilda in Manchester.

Since Hilda has been at Fletcher House she has felt safe, knowing there is always someone there if she needs anything. Her laugh resounds around the home and she is loved by everyone. She doesn't always need to talk and sometimes just likes to sit with the sun on her face, lost in thought. Just knowing there's a friendly face and that someone may just wander over and say hello or give her a hug, brightens her day. She feels that at Fletcher House people really care and that means the world to her.

FLORENCE YELLAND

'I've always loved dancing – I wish I had been able to have lessons'

FLORENCE WAS BORN in Bridgwater on December 2nd 1910. The fourth of six children, Florence had two older brothers (Cecil and Fred), an older sister (Winnie) and two younger siblings. Her father Clifford Baker was an engineer at Wills' factories but in his spare time he enjoyed coaching rugby and football, helping to patch up cuts and bruises, and bandage sprained ankles. Florence's mother often complained that at times her front room was like a doctor's surgery! The garden was long and narrow with a menagerie of different birds. Clifford fancied himself as a pigeon racer and would compete against his friends on Saturday afternoons but he also kept fowl at the bottom of the garden and a familiar clucking would ring out when it was time to roast a bird on a Sunday. Florence's mother had been an apprentice dressmaker until she married but now looked after the family, which usually meant keeping the purse strings drawn tight. The Yellands had always rented their house and often Florence was sent to pay one and sixpence to Mr Palmer the landlord. Florence's three religious spinster aunts made up the family and they were happy – working class and proud of it.

Florence went to St Mary's school and she and her friends would huddle together, giggling at the boys who were cockily strolling through the gates of Dr Morgan's School across the road. She was very sporty and loved running, looking forward to sports day so that she could take part in the different races that were set on the rugby field. She was also very keen on classical dance. Her mother wanted to send her to dance lessons but these had to stop due to the cost. She was prepared to be patient while her two brothers were doing their apprenticeships, as when they had completed them they would find jobs and there would be more money in the pot. That was not to be the case however as they both got married. To this day Florence still wishes she had been able to take dance classes and loves to watch the dancing on television on Saturday nights.

When she left school Florence went to work at the Wyatt & Hegart shirt factory. She would walk to work from Avonmouth Road to Blacklands, taking care not to be late as they shut the gates if you were not on time and you lost a day's pay. She had got the job through a friend of her mother's who owned an army surplus shop in town, and she was allowed to keep most of what she earned. It was mostly women on the shop floor as the men tended to look after the machinery and everyone worked from 9 am until 4.30pm. The forewoman was called Nell, a

D.O.B. 02/12/1910

135

Two young ladies
walking across
Bridgwater Town
Bridge circa 1930.

Stillmans 2011.

robust red-cheeked woman with a glint in her eye. She was strict but fair and would dock staff four and sixpence if their stitching was wrong.

It was the mid 1920s and when the girls had spare time they all got together and went for a day out over Wembdon Hill. They travelled in a horse and cart as this was long before the Quantock Road was built. They also went dancing to Blake Hall which cost sixpence, and Florence would sit with a glass of orange and listen to Bobby Gray striking the piano keys. Every so often a boy would ask for a dance and the girls giddily moved to the foxtrot or the lancers. It was at one of these dances that Florence used her 'ladies excuse me' to ask a boy to dance. His name was Mervyn and he nervously followed as she led him around the dance floor. All her girlfriends had laughed as she had always insisted that the boy for her would have to dance. They courted for many years before finally Florence plucked up the courage and said, "I've had this ring on my finger for 8 years, isn't it about time we got married?". They were married in 1936 at Trinity Church which has since been pulled down to build the Broadway, and had their reception in a pub called the Mansion House which was run by Gertie Miller, an old friend of her parents. The happy couple moved into a small rented room off the Staplegrove Road on the outskirts of Taunton, and with a little help from his parents and what Mervyn earned as a telephone engineer, they started to build a life for themselves.

In 1938, whilst staying with her mother-in-law Lavinia and while Mervyn was on a course in London, Florence gave birth to a baby girl called Patricia. Florence and Lavinia had had a difficult relationship for many years, as Florence considered Lavinia to be domineering and jealous of her marriage to her son. This was to be exacerbated by the arrival of a thrilled new father, rushing home from London to see his baby daughter. Instead of Lavinia opening the door and allowing Florence to greet her husband with the baby in her arms, she made Florence answer the door and handed her son the baby. Florence would never forgive her for this. Just before the outbreak of war the family finally moved into a small friendly cul-de-sac on the outskirts of Taunton and settled into a new life, unaware of the challenges and dangers ahead.

As Mervyn's job was seen as a reserve occupation Florence was lucky to have her husband at home, and he would travel to work or to his Home Guard duties on his motorbike while Florence stayed at home with the baby, soaking nappies and making bubbling pots of stew. As times were hard they had to make everything stretch. Florence had a nice surprise one day when she went into Stillman's the local butchers thinking she would have to buy a tiny piece of gammon and Miss Wilson came out of the back room and pushed a paper parcel into her shopping bag. When she got home she found a huge breast of lamb which she used to make Mervyn a mouth watering Irish Stew that lasted the whole week.

During the war if you had a spare room it was quite likely that you might either have an evacuee or an American soldier billeted to your house. Florence had two charming Americans stay with her for some time and they remained firm friends for many years. Sargeant Sandy Shafts was a fairhaired big built man while Corporal Gerald Ducey was small and dark, and Florence recalls them scooping up sweet rations and chocolate bars from the naffy at Norton Fitzwarren with which they would fill little Patricia's apron. She remembers the joy on the boys' faces at being given half an English egg with a slightly runny golden yolk and she smiles broadly as she says, "they used to think the world of me." Over the years she often wondered how they were and the family not only received letters but when their daughters were old enough, one of them came to visit Florence. She had never seen a robin until one flew onto Florence's kitchen windowsill.

THE GI!! THE AMERICAN SOLDIER DURING WWII

On December 7th 1941 the Imperial Japanese Army launched a surprise military attack on the US naval base at Pearl Harbour, Hawaii. Soon after this America entered the war and a steady trickle of American soldiers began to arrive in Britain; a mixture of fervent volunteer kids, older draftees, soldiers, sailors, marines from the Iowa cornfields and an airman from a Detroit assembly line. A patch on the left shoulder showed the division in which he served. One of the earliest units to arrive in England was the 34th 'Red Bull' Infantry Division. At first the Americans decided to concentrate on building up air power, giving them time to train and mobilise their other forces. Approximately 30,000 American airmen flying from British airbases died during World War II and the countryside of Britain was dotted with over 700 airbases, out of which flew RAF and USAAF fighters and bombers.

After the war ended Patricia went to school in North Town, Mervyn continued working for the telephone exchange, and Florence enjoyed cooking and looking after her family. Over the next few years Florence and Mervyn were happy and content and she would look back on this time and feel glad that she had asked the shy boy with two left feet to dance.

The first signs of multiple sclerosis started to show in the mid 1950s as Mervyn started to complain of numbness in his hands and slightly distorted sight. In time his mobility was greatly affected. Mervyn would see the doctor coming down the road and be scared and Florence would say, "They'll never take you, Mervyn, not while I've got two hands". There were very many visits to the hospital but there was very little help and support for this condition at the time.

During this time Florence was supported by Patricia, who was still living at home and the family would go on day trips to places like Burnham on Sea. The biggest treat was buying crusty rolls from a local baker and a bag of shrimps and sitting on the sand, pinching and pulling the soft pink shells. They also enjoyed taking the train to Blue Anchor and for a while they had a holiday chalet in Seaton. Mervyn wasn't very mobile but these trips gave them the chance to be together as a family, and Florence relished every moment she had with him. Mervyn passed away in 1969 and Florence never fell in love again.

Blue Anchor.

Even though they lived fairly near to each other the Yellands were not a very close family. Uncle Fred ran a Newsagents' shop on West Street, Florence's sister Ida ran the Bath Bridge Inn and they went to Auntie Win's on a Saturday. There might be a whist drive on a Wednesday and sometimes they went to Lavinia's on a Friday for a smoked fish supper. Social occasions aside there didn't seem to be that much support for Florence during this time. In the aftermath of Mervyn's death, Florence and Patricia clung together and started to create a new bond. They also found a new mutual interest and started to travel around the world and Florence, who had never flown before, absolutely loved it. They went on a variety of package holidays to places like Austria, Italy and Spain. After Pat was married they went to Canada twice, staying in a bungalow on the St Lawrence River or with cousins in Toronto. The memory of a breathtaking visit to the Rockies is still in Florence's mind now.

THE ERA OF THE PACKAGE HOLIDAY

In the 'ration book' Britain of the 1950s, the holiday represented a great temptation and a good investment as the travel brochure promised "they would sleep under canvas, enjoy delicious meat-filled meals and as much local wine as they could drink and would have return flights all for the all inclusive price of £32.10s."

The first form of package was organised by Thomas Cook in 1841, offering customers a return trip between Leicester and Loughborough. He trumped this in 1855 with the first package tour of Europe when he took a group from Leicester to Calais to coincide with the Paris Exhibition. By the 1860s he was taking groups to Switzerland, Egypt, Italy and America, establishing a new form of 'inclusive independent travel', letting the traveller retain their independence while an agency charged for travel, food and accommodation over a fixed period.

In the 1950s Vladamir Raitz pioneered the first mass package holiday abroad, flying from Gatwick to Corsica and later to Palma and the Costa Brava. He set up Horizon Holidays after the realisation that he could charter an aircraft providing an all inclusive two week holiday for less than £35. The name Horizon was chosen to reflect the blue horizon that passengers would see from a plane window. This was a revelation to the British as it gave most people the chance to have affordable holidays abroad and people continued to enjoy this way of travelling throughout the 1950s and 1960s, with mass tourism opening up in places such as Crete and the Algarve.

The industry went into decline in the Seventies, experiencing difficulties due to the rise of budget airlines, the first being Freddie Laker's Sky Train service between London and New York in the late 1970s. People were also now independently sourcing and planning their own trips. The trend saw a comeback in 2009 as many holiday and flight companies went into liquidation and the 'hidden' costs of 'no frills' airlines increased.

In 1972 Patricia was married in St Andrew's church in Taunton and there were tears in her eyes as her Uncle Cecil gave her away. After Patricia married, she and Geoff moved to Kent and only visited once a month. Florence had more time alone and tried to fill her days as much as possible to stop her thinking sad thoughts. Just around the corner lived an old friend Mrs Darch and Florence often sat with her and her husband in the evenings, watching television or sifting through bric a brac for the church sale. She also treasures the memory of a trip to Blackpool with her sister-in-law Ethel and how they went to the Empress Ballroom at the Winter Gardens to watch the dancing.

BLACKPOOL AND CLASSICAL DANCE

The sheer size and grandeur of the Empress Ballroom is astounding. The ballroom was completed during the summer of 1896 and had a floor area of 12,500 sq. ft. It is one of the largest ballrooms in the world and was also used to assemble gas envelopes for the R.33 airship during WWI.

The Blackpool Dance Festival began during the Easter week of 1920 in the impressive Empress Ballroom of the Winter Gardens. In those days the dances in the ballrooms consisted mainly of Sequence Waltzes, Two Steps, the Lancers and novelty dances. As modern ballroom and Latin American dance had not yet evolved, the festival was devoted to finding new Sequence dances in three tempos: the Waltz, Two Step and Foxtrot. This format continued until the early 1930s when dancing began to change and there was a general interest in the developing 'English Style' of dancing, with newly titled Championships and preliminary heats held across the country with the winners dancing at the Grand Final in Blackpool.

During WWII everything closed down only to reopen in 1946, and due to the resurgence and popularity of the Sequence competitions the Winter Gardens held an Old Time Ball in 1950. Towards the 1960s there was an influx of foreign competitors and in the last few years no less than 50 different countries have been represented, with the introduction of Latin American dancing making a great impact on the dancing world.

Sydenham House, 2011.

In 1975 Patricia gave birth to a daughter, Lisa, and when she was 18 months old Patricia moved back to Bridgwater. She bought a big house and took over the newsagents from her uncle Fred and for the next few years Florence had her family close by again. With the addition of a new granddaughter, family occasions became big joyous affairs again. The festive season was always spent together with the family going to the Yellands in Taunton on Christmas Day where a goose held centre stage and on Boxing Day they went to Grandma Baker in Bridgwater to play cards and eat cold turkey and piccalilli sandwiches.

Florence finally left Draycott Avenue in 1988 as Patricia worried far too much about her being on her own. Florence was to live with Patricia for the next 20 years. She had her own comfortable sitting room and a lovely summer house in the garden to sit in. Patricia cooked in the evenings and Florence would join them for dinner. The whole family also organised a fabulous surprise party for Florence's 90th birthday with lots of relatives, sparkling wine and a lavish meal. Although she was happy and grateful that her daughter was sharing her home with her, it was not like having a companion. She missed her husband and when the end of the evening came and Patricia and Geoff went to their own room, Florence felt a void that was impossible to fill. Since losing Mervyn, Florence had packed her life with as much as she could to stop herself feeling lonely but although they did everything they could for her, the time spent at Northfield was a mixture of happy and sad times.

Patricia became concerned about Florence's health as she was not very mobile and had fallen out of bed on more than one occasion. It was terrifying to hear a bang and a crash in the middle of the night. Florence was admitted to hospital for a short while as there were not adequate nursing facilities in Patricia's house. Florence has now been at Sydenham House for 2 years and feels a lot safer, as all she has to do if she needs help is press a button and someone will be there. The warmth and comfort provided by the carers is a small thing but it brightens up Florence's day.

HARRY PATCH

'Just an ordinary man'

D.O.B. 17/06/1898

HARRY PATCH TOUCHED the hearts of many. One such person was his friend Nick Fear, who had known Harry for over 10 years when he passed away, and remembers him fondly. Nick's grandfather was a Lewis gunner and he was always interested to meet people who had used the same weapon. Nick attended a talk which Harry gave at Bridgwater Police Station one afternoon, and found him to be a fascinating and captivating man. From here a close friendship developed between the two men, both Bathonians who were born in Coombe Down. Nick, along with another of Harry's friends, Jim Ross, saw the real Harry Patch and have shared their memories.

Harry became famous for the thing he didn't want to be known for – as a soldier in the First World War. There were many epithets in Harry's life: a son; a chorister; a husband; a brother; a father; a plumber; and for a short time, a soldier. There was so much more to Harry, yet he always carried the painful memories within him. He was a deep thinking man, and on occasion would feel deeply unhappy as a memory was triggered. On certain days Nick would visit him and ask, "How are you today, Harry?" and his reply would be, "Well I'm ok!" yet sometimes the most innocuous question about the weather or "How's your day?" was met with a look, and he would ponder the question for a moment and say, "Well, I take each day as it comes … just like when we were at Passchendaele!"

Fletcher House had a date and a name circled in the diary - Harry Patch, October 21 1996. Harry had lived alone in a bungalow in Wells since his wife passed away and was good friends with Betty and Fred Isaacs. They had known each other for years and when Fred said, "If I die, can you look after Betty?" Harry agreed. He may have remained independent for longer but when Betty decided to move (complete with her cats), Harry kept his promise and followed. And so it was that Fletcher House became Harry's home.

When Harry first moved to Fletcher House, the memories of Pilkem Ridge had been buried for many years. He had a room in the old part of the building and there were glass panels over his door that let in 'saved light'. Opposite Harry's door was a linen store and when the door was opened during the night by the carers, it caused the neon light to flash. This took Harry right back to Pilkem Ridge.

There came a time in Harry's life when he felt the need to confront his demons. As one of the very few remaining of the generation, Harry was approached by television companies who wanted

Preparing for an interview.

Harry and Doris at Fletcher House.

Harry and Doris off for a drive.

him to tell his story, and he started to open up and talk about his war and his emotions. He never wanted to go back to the battlefields although he knew it was the only way he would exorcise the ghosts. The first time he went back to Pilkem Ridge he was so overcome that he couldn't get off the coach and wept for all those who would never see their wife's face or the sun rise, pale red in a morning sky. But he faced his demons and said the oration under the Menin Gate.

Nick remembers a poignant moment from one of Harry's visits to the battlefields. It was a gloomy day and the light was fading. The BBC were filming and there was a strange atmosphere of calm. Harry wanted to place a wreath on the divisional memorial and as he did so there was a shaft of light on the back of his head and on the note on the wreath, although when the film was cut there was no sign of the light. There was a tremendous sense of peace for Harry, as he felt that he had laid a ghost to rest. From being so reticent about sharing his experiences, Harry now wanted to do many things to share the story of the true horror of war.

As much as Harry had dreaded returning to the battlefields, so he dreaded meeting a German. This changed in November 2004 when Harry met Charles Kuentz, a German soldier from the Western Front. Both men were pacifists and the first time they met, Harry placed a wreath on an unknown soldier's grave with Charles. Nick was with Harry before he met Charles Kuentz and noticed Harry sitting thoughtfully, with his hands clasped as if in prayer. He turned to Nick and said, "Do you reckon this man is the man I shot?" remembering the German he had left on the battlefield. Although this was unlikely, Harry also knew Charles may have fired the whiz-bang that created his horrors, but admitted that, even if this proved to be the case, he would still have shaken hands with him.

Harry's fame came when he reached 100 and people realised he was one of the last remaining veterans of the First World War. He became a national hero and thrived on having a full social diary. He enjoyed being recognised when going to the bank in Wells or to the gardens of the Bishop's Palace, and would look up proudly when somebody said, "Are you Harry Patch?" Harry started getting mail from all over the world, some weeks receiving over 100 letters, and although he wanted to reply to each one it proved difficult due to his arthritis. There was something about Harry that struck a chord with people and his celebrity status had many rewards: on one occasion he was reunited with a niece in Devon; schoolchildren wrote and sent him beautifully decorated cards; and a very special cider, Patch's Pride, was made for his 104th birthday, with the brewer sending him 104 bottles which were distributed amongst family, friends and staff at Fletcher House. Harry was also able to impart his pearls of wisdom as he became an agony uncle for *FHM* magazine although he disliked the sepia tinted photograph, thinking it aged him. He donated his earnings to the residents' fund box at Fletcher House as he couldn't imagine a more worthy recipient, and the money paid for days out to places like Burrington Combe and provided a piano for the home.

The staff at Fletcher House had always been supportive, and when Betty passed away they provided all the sympathy and warmth that Harry needed. When he felt ready to move on he met a lady called Doris Whittaker who had moved into Fletcher House when her husband died. When Harry went into town he would return with a red rose or a box of chocolates for Doris and when they sat together in the dining room at Fletcher House, the fading light created an odd picture of something quite unreal. Nick felt as if a bright light surrounded them and if you could paint emotion, well, all you had to do was look at Doris's face and the love between them.

Nick visited Harry regularly and they would drive around the lanes of Somerset, visiting Harry's old haunts. There were certain places that brought back long forgotten memories. Harry used to live in a beautiful thatched cottage in the village of Compton Dundon, between Street and Somerton, and he revisited the cottage on several occasions, once being invited in for tea. During the war many army units were located in the fields that surrounded these Somerset villages and Harry managed some of these camps for the British Army, the US Tank Corps and US Army, being responsible for all the plumbing. On many of these drives Harry would point at a field and turn to Nick and say, "There was a search light battery there and just over there was a shed with a toilet in it", and Nick saw an empty field with some cows in the far corner. It made him realise that the past has left a ghostly outline on so much we take for granted.

Fletcher House treats everyone as an individual, making each resident feel special. There are occasions where birthday parties and celebrations are a time for everyone to come together but the home understands that each resident has their own needs and if somebody wants to be alone, they can be. The home has a reputation for wonderful food and homemade cakes but if a resident wants their meal in their room or a sandwich instead, the staff are more than happy to accommodate. When Harry came back home after a long day, all he wanted was to be tucked up in bed, warm and satisfied, with a sandwich and a cup of cocoa. He was looked after impeccably, always having clean clothes and an immaculate shave. It was the little touches that made Harry's stay at Fletcher so happy. He had a double room with a settee and when the time came to decorate and fit a brand new carpet, he gave permission. Whilst rearranging his room, the workmen removed the sink from the middle of the room and fitted a new one in the corner. Harry was unhappy about this change in his routine as he had used the sink to steady himself and when the staff realised he was unhappy, they moved it back. These are the lengths that Fletcher House goes to in order to keep every resident happy. People cared for him because he was Harry Patch the resident, not the celebrity.

On one occasion a rock band came to Fletcher House, wanting Harry to speak the words of the oration', so they could use it as an introduction to a song. This reminded Harry of someone in his past who had also said it.

The Reverend Tubby Clayton took his faith very seriously. He was a first class officer but also a clergyman who converted an old hop house into an organisation called Talbot House about 15 miles behind the front line. He realised that the morals of the local people were not good and the soldiers were being dragged down, so he created an environment of peace and calm in the midst of chaos. Talbot House was a wonderful institution and a place where you could go and have a cup of tea and escape the war for a while before going back to the trenches. At the top of the building was a chapel and he gave communion to the soldiers, to men who may not come back. Tubby Clayton said the oration on the morning of September 22 1917 and gave Harry and his comrades their last communion.

Another person who was close to Harry at Fletcher House was the Manager Carol Mohide, who often acted as a buffer between Harry and the media. She was always there when he needed his shoes polished for an important visit, and protected his dignity when the press were around and he need to be transferred from a wheelchair to a chair. The last couple of years were very intense. He wore his medals with pride every single day and he would choose what he wanted to say and then gave Carol a look that said, "I've had enough!" with the pain clearly etched on his face.

Another friend, Jim Ross, shared a memory of Harry which showed his sense of humour. Harry

Harry celebrating his 108th birthday at Fletcher House enjoying a special cake.

Harry Patch celebrating his 110th birthday.

Carole Mohide receiving the Harry Patch award, 2009.

With Poet Laureate
Andrew Motion.

Saying goodbye,
August 2009.

was to appear at the Cenotaph with fellow World War One veterans Bill Stone and Henry Allingham to commemorate the 90th anniversary of the armistice. Harry didn't want to go up to London the night before. Better by far to sleep in his own bed and make an early start. Jim's instructions having been given, he then commenced detailed instructions with the Ministry of Defence who organise such ceremonies. At all costs, Harry had to be there on time. And the only way to get him through central London was with a police motorcycle escort. The MOD pulled strings and the motorbikes appeared and whisked the limousine through central London in a blur of red lights and startled motorists. As Jim, Harry, and Jim's wife sped past Harrods at 60 mph on the wrong side of the road Harry was asked if he was aware of just how many laws were being broken. "Oh yes" he said, turning round with a smile which stretched from one ear to the other. That was Harry the ordinary man. One hour later he was representing his generation.

Towards the end of Harry's life, he became frail and weak. Nick's last memory of Harry is in the Chapel of Rest, where he lay dressed in pyjamas and a silk dressing gown, with perfectly combed hair and a posy of flowers. Nobody would have known that that was what he wanted but the wonderful carers at Fletcher House knew.

Harry's funeral was a public affair, held at Wells Cathedral with the Head of the Armed Forces and Camilla Parker Bowles among invited guests. Jim Ross, wrote and delivered the eulogy from which the following lines are taken …

'Creating images which are seared on our minds
The last Tommy clutching a wreath for his mates
Every life! All their lives were precious to him
They were all victims.

We are the ordinary ones.
Harry was the extraordinary man
The plumber from Combe Down
Who showed us true heroism
Now, at long long last, Harry, you can rest in peace.'

Harry's 'real' funeral was at Monkton Combe (Harry's local church was at Combe Down, but burials weren't allowed there as there were quarries underneath) and only a select few were invited including many of the staff from Fletcher House. The cemetery at Monkton Combe is where Harry's parents, grandparents, great grandparents, brothers and aunts are buried and he visited his parents' grave often. Harry is now home with his family, or standing on top of Wrekin Hill, holding Ada's hand.

Harry wanted to be remembered for peace and reconciliation and if he was speaking to us from beyond the grave, he might be worried about being called 'The Last Tommy'. It wasn't that he minded the name, but he may not have wanted that to be how he was remembered. And maybe it is time to draw a line under the fact that he was a soldier, as every single boy was a soldier.

Harry was honoured by the King of Belgium, the President of France and the people of Britain. He accepted these honours with great humility, for he knew they were his only by reason of his great age. He knew he was just an ordinary man.